PRAISE FOR GLENN PATTERSON

'One of the fatal flaws of the Brexit project was wilful igno-
rance about Northern Ireland, its border with the Republic
of Ireland, and the historic entanglements that made a "clean
break" from the EU impossible. Combining the vividness and
humour of the novelist with the insight and astuteness of the
analyst, Glenn Patterson unties all the knots and infuses the
history with the humanity of lived experience.

As a guide for the bewildered, *Backstop Land* is a great place
to start. As a plea for understanding and care, it reminds us of
where we should hope to end up. Funny, wise, entertaining
and illuminating, this book is one of the best things to come
out of the Brexit saga.'

FINTAN O'TOOLE, ON *BACKSTOP LAND*

'*The International* is an act of courage. It is the best book about
the Troubles ever written.'

ANNE ENRIGHT, ON *THE INTERNATIONAL*

'Glenn Patterson has become the most serious and humane
chronicler of Northern Ireland over the past thirty years, as
well as one of the best contemporary Irish novelists.'

COLM TÓIBÍN, ON *THE INTERNATIONAL*

BACKSTOP LAND

GLENN PATTERSON

BACKSTOP LAND

HEAD
of ZEUS

An Apollo Book

This is an Apollo book, first published in the UK in 2019
by Head of Zeus Ltd

9 7 5 3 1 2 4 6 8

A catalogue record for this book is available from
the British Library.

ISBN (FTPO): 9781838932022
ISBN (E): 9781838932039

Typeset by Adrian McLaughlin

Printed and bound in Great Britain by
CPI Group (UK) Ltd, Croydon CR0 4YY

Head of Zeus Ltd
First Floor East
5–8 Hardwick Street
London ECIR 4RG

WWW.HEADOFZEUS.COM

Contents

'Nobody knows anything.'

William Goldman, *Adventures in the Screen Trade*

'No Government should commit a country to a course of action in which the consequences were so opaque as to be incalculable.'

Right Reverend John McDowell, Bishop of Clogher[1]

'The philosophical conservative is someone willing to pay the price of other people's suffering for his principles.'

E. L. Doctorow

'Where we live is basically a piss-take of the world.'

Scott McKendry, Sunflower Bar, 11 June 2019

This is kind of personal

Chronology

1600s   Plantation of Ulster. Derry (Irish Doire, Oak Grove) acquires a *London*; Counties Antrim and Down, lots and lots of Scots. (Some – Protestant – people would tell you they were just returning home.)

1690   Battle of the Boyne (1 July, adjusted to 12 July, by adoption of Gregorian Calendar). The Protestant William of Orange defeats Catholic James II: a big European war with very long-term, local consequences.

1795   One of those local consequences: Orange Order formed in County Armagh.

1798   United Irishmen's Rebellion – Catholic, Protestant, Dissenter... who ended up fighting one another, if not always in the combinations expected. (The mainly Catholic Monaghan Militia fought with the British Army against mainly Protestant rebels in Ballynahinch, County Down.)

1800   Act of Union, creating the United Kingdom of Great Britain and Ireland and a flag of many crosses.

1886   First Home Rule Bill, to give Ireland a measure of self-government (still within the UK). To adherents of the Union – 'Unionists' – Home Rule was Rome Rule.

1905   Sinn Féin formed.

1912   Third Home Rule Bill passed; a 'Solemn League and Covenant' signed by 471,414 (mainly Ulster) people to resist it.

1913   At the start of the year, formation of the Ulster Volunteer
Force; at the end of the year, formation of the Irish
Volunteer Force (imitation, flattery etc.).

1914   Outbreak of the First World War. Home Rule Act put on
ice. UVF morphs into 36th (Ulster) Division. Many Irish
Catholics as well as Protestants join the 16th (Irish) Division.

1916   April, Easter Rising by Irish Volunteers and Irish Citizen's
Army directed by the smaller secret Irish Republican
Brotherhood; Declaration of the Irish Republic; 1 July, first
day of Battle of the Somme: 36th (Ulster) Division suffers
heavy casualties.

1919   January, Meeting of First Dáil Éireann: Seventy-three Sinn
Féin MPs, abstaining from Westminster, sit in Dublin; same
day, first Irish Republican Army action (they were still calling
themselves 'Volunteers'): the theft of dynamite and the
murder of two police constables at Soloheadbeg, County
Tipperary.

1920   Government of Ireland Act: in effect a fourth Home Rule
Bill, with separate parliaments in the new (six-county)
Northern Ireland, at Stormont, and the (twenty-six-county)
Irish Free State of Ireland.

1922   Partition comes into effect. That strange wee wiggly line.

1949   The Free State (having tried out Dominion status from 1937)
declares itself the fully independent Republic of Ireland,
with a territorial claim to Northern Ireland.

1956   Without being asked by anyone, the IRA enacts its own territorial claim with the 'Border Campaign' to drive Britain out of Ireland. It doesn't. Campaign ends in 1962. IRA takes a leftward turn in the aftermath.

1966   50th anniversary of the Easter Rising followed by 50th anniversary of the Somme. Unionist fears of renewed IRA activity stoked by Revd Ian Paisley, whose Ulster Protestant Volunteers collegiately shares a motto with the reformed UVF, which in early summer of that year carries out three murders in Belfast.

1967   Northern Ireland Civil Rights Association (NICRA) formed in Belfast's International Hotel.

1968   5 October: a NICRA demonstration in Derry is broken up by police in full view of TV cameras. Never was 'ugly scenes' more apt.

1969   Unrest worsens despite attempts by Unionist government to introduce reforms (too little too late for Nationalists, altogether too much for 'Paisleyites'); August, 'Battle of the Bogside' in Derry is followed by even worse rioting in Belfast, with whole streets burned and seven people killed, including nine-year-old Patrick Rooney, struck by a bullet from a heavy-duty machine gun, mounted on a police armoured car. (That a UK police force even *had* heavy-duty machine guns and armoured cars...) British troops arrive. And stay for nearly thirty years.

1970   Easter Rising commemoration: the first public demonstration of the split in the IRA. Supporters of the 'Official' IRA – accused of leaving Catholic areas of Belfast undefended in its embrace of Marxist politics – wear stick-on Easter Lily emblems to the commemoration and are henceforth

'Stickies'. The rival, more militant Provisional IRA (Provos or Provies), formed in December 1969, very quickly comes to dominate. Alliance Party formed. Domination slower. Social Democratic and Labour Party formed.

1971   9 August, Stormont government introduces internment. Despite the fact that loyalists are active and killing, only republicans are targeted. September, Ulster Defence Association formed from Protestant vigilante groups; Democratic Unionist Party formed.

1972   30 January, a NICRA anti-internment march in Derry ends with members of the Parachute Regiment shooting dead thirteen unarmed men – seven of them teenagers. A fourteenth dies of his injuries. 'Bloody Sunday' leads to scores rushing to join the IRA. According to David Ervine, later leader of the Progressive Unionist Party, 'Bloody Friday', on 21 July, in which nine people were killed in at least twenty IRA bombs across Belfast, led him to join the UVF. In between those two Bloody events the Westminster government prorogued the Northern Ireland government at Stormont and imposed Direct Rule.

1973   8 March, Border Poll: 98.9 per cent to 1.1 per cent in favour of remaining in the UK; cf. 21 November, Chile 1 USSR 0 (the USSR didn't turn up; neither did the nationalist part of the Northern Ireland electorate in March); 9 December, Sunningdale Agreement: hello power-sharing (mark 1).

1974   May, Ulster Workers' Council Strike (bye-bye power-sharing mark 1); also in May loyalist bombs in Dublin and Monaghan kill thirty-four, including a full-term unborn child. December, another split in the Official IRA produces, in quick succession, the Irish Republican Socialist Party and the Irish National Liberation Army, which itself later splits to produce the Irish People's Liberation Organization.

1976   End of Special Category Status for paramilitary prisoners: start of 'blanket protest' by republican prisoners, who refused to wear prison uniform.

1979   27 August, Narrow Water ambush: sixteen members of the Parachute Regiment and two other soldiers killed in double bomb-blast: largest single loss of life for British Army in Northern Ireland; the IRA had earlier that day killed Lord Mountbatten, Prince Philip's uncle, with a bomb in his boat off the coast of Sligo.

1981   The prison protests escalate to a hunger strike in which ten republican prisoners die, the first being Bobby Sands, elected MP for Fermanagh and South Tyrone shortly before his death. Signals start of 'armalite and ballot box' strategy, a turn to politics with no let-up in the armed campaign.

1985   Anglo-Irish Agreement gives Irish government a limited input into Northern Irish affairs. Paisley tells a huge crowd in Belfast he will not accept it: 'Never! Never! Never!' (Scroll down to 2006.)

1986   Republican Sinn Féin formed after split over Sinn Féin's ending of abstentionism in the South. As is customary they almost at once start a new (Continuity) IRA.

1987   8 November, the Provisionals carry on with their campaign to unite the people of Ireland by killing eleven Protestants gathering for a Remembrance Day service in Enniskillen,

County Fermanagh. (A twelfth died thirteen years later without ever emerging from a coma.)

1988 May, three unarmed IRA members shot out of hand on the streets of Gibraltar; three mourners killed in a loyalist attack on the funeral, in Milltown cemetery, of one of the victims; two British Army corporals dragged from a car and killed at the funeral of one of the Milltown victims. The priest who knelt by them and prayed as they died carried in his pocket a communiqué from Gerry Adams to John Hume, leader of the SDLP: one of the first acts in the process leading to...

1994 31 August, first Provisional IRA ceasefire; 13 October, Loyalist ceasefire.

1996 End of IRA ceasefire signalled by massive bomb in London's Docklands.

1997 19 July, start of the next ceasefire. Real IRA splits from Provisionals.

1998 10 April, Belfast (aka Good Friday) Agreement, endorsed by 71.12 per cent of the Northern Ireland electorate; August, Real IRA bomb in Omagh kills twenty-nine people and unborn twins.

1999 Northern Ireland Assembly meets for the first time.

2000 Northern Ireland Assembly suspended for the first time.

2001 Northern Ireland Assembly suspended twice more (twenty-four hours each).

2002–07 Northern Ireland Assembly suspended for a really, really long time.

2006 St Andrews Agreement. The DUP and Sinn Féin become partners in government; Dublin's role far greater than

anything envisaged in Anglo-Irish Agreement. Paisley: 'Nev–
... Ah, all right then.'

2012   New IRA formed out of bits of Old IRA.

2014   Stormont House Agreement, designed to reach accommodation on issues outstanding from St Andrews, of identity,
the past, flags, parades and the Irish language.

2015   Fresh Start Agreement (what you end up with after you
add ten weeks of talks to Stormont House).

2016   EU Referendum: 56 per cent of Northern Irish voters back
Remain.

2017   Northern Ireland Assembly suspended for the – what's
that? – sixth time (ongoing).

2018   November, EU and UK government agree final terms of
'backstop' proposal. In order to keep the border between
both parts of Ireland open, the UK will remain in a Customs
Union until something better can be thrashed out. (The
alternative 'border in the Irish Sea' is even more ghastly to
Unionists, on both sides of that sea.)

2019   18 April, the New IRA murders journalist and LGBT rights
campaigner Lyra McKee in Derry, bringing to over 160 the
number of paramilitary-related murders since the Good
Friday Agreement.

Speech

This is the prime manister speakin.
Know what yer aw thinkin.
How ma goin tay sort oot the boarder
noo wi Breggsit an aw?
Mtellinye dinny worry.
Won't be plain sailin
but fAh could jist explain.
There's nuthin tay worry aboot.

We don know yet fthere'll be
a clean Breggsit ra messy Breggsit
nur a hard Breggsit nur a saft Breggsit.
But mnot goin te build a hard boarder.
It'll be a soft boarder, waitn see.
A sorta magic boarder that no-one can see.
We can hay a boarder that isny a boarder.
One tay keep youse in, an everyone else oot.

We can hay loadsa jobs on the boarder.
Know checkin passports, customs, makin fences,
driving diggers tay dig up roads
n puttin boulders an aw the wee small roads
that's jist been opened up agin not longsince.
Won't be goin back tay the old days, not at aw.
Lotsa opportunaties. Wee businesses, know,
filling stayshuns n fegs n booze n that,
know, tea shaps an bars an that kinda thing.
Goin tay stayshun controlsn the portsn airports
n thi Republic, workin wi the Irish government.
Know they're independent noo but

listen, just cos Ah tawk posh
disny mean Ah dinny unnerstan yer feelins.
Ah was an em pee fur a lang time
fore Ah was the pee em. We wul sort it.
How? I dinny know but ock it'll be awright.
Quit gernin. What's that?
Ah canny unnerstan anybody
who tawks like that.
Youse r naw makin sense.

Elaine Gaston

Prologue

Friday, 9 June 2017. I am in London with my friend and screen-writing partner, Colin Carberry, talking to the producers of a couple of films we are working on. Both, as it happens, musical biopics – an area where (in truth, the only area where) we have a bit of form, having co-written *Good Vibrations*, based on, as we were careful to say, the 'true stories' of legendary Belfast record-shop owner, inveterate yarn-spinner and perpetual contrarian, Terri Hooley.

Musicals are having a moment. *La La Land* is still in its first flush and Rob Marshall's *Mary Poppins Returns* is filming at Shepperton Studios, sixteen miles down the road from where Colin and I are having our meetings.

Yesterday, Thursday, 8 June, the United Kingdom of Great Britain and Northern Ireland went to the polls, in a general election called just two months before and against all expectation by Prime Minister Theresa May (already that feels like writing 'Anthony Eden'), in a bid to strengthen her hand within parliament and her own party ahead of Brexit negotiations with Brussels. The election had taken the Conservatives from 330 seats – an overall majority of four – to just 317, nine short of the number needed to govern without the support of other parties.

The Northern Ireland electorate, meantime, with no Labour or Liberal Democratic candidates to choose from, and only a very small field of Conservatives, had returned seven Sinn Féin MPs (who had run, as was their wont, on an abstentionist ticket, that is, a promise not to take any seats they won) and from the Democratic Unionist Party (DUP), the only Northern Irish party to have backed Leave in the United Kingdom European Union Membership Referendum the year before, *ten* MPs.

It had become starkly apparent by the time Colin and I stepped off the early Friday morning plane from Belfast that the fate of Theresa May's government – the whole tenor of the UK's departure from the European Union – depended on a single Northern Irish party. Not just any Northern Irish party, *that* Northern Irish party, with its eccentric views on all manner of things, from same-sex relationships to the origins of the universe. (Though, in true DUP negotiation style, the pact that the Tories sought would not be reached until seventeen days later and even then would take the form of a 'confidence and supply' arrangement rather than formal coalition: the government would have to keep coming back to seek their support.)

The people we were meeting were by turns baffled and affronted. 'Who the fuck are these people?'

And they weren't the only ones. The question dogged Colin and me every step of our day.

They were asking it in shops – who the fuck are they?

They were asking it in bars – who the fuck are they?

They were asking it on the streets – who the fuck are they? – and out the windows of cars – who the fuck are they?

If we had been writing it as a musical, the billposter sliding down his ladder would have been asking it, over his shoulder – who the fuck are they? The faces on the bill he had just finished posting would have been asking it and everyone would have laughed, short and sharp, taking the number up another notch – full-blown *Mary Poppins Returns* style, drone's-eye view, upper windows thrown wide open, half a million of them maybe, one for every person who in the next forty-eight hours would sign a petition calling on the Tories not to do a deal – Who the fuck are they? Who the fuck are they? – building and building to a surround-sound crescendo.

Just – who – the – fuck – are – they?

And then a pause in which Colin and I looked at one another, shrugged, and turned to the camera and sang our first and only line… 'Welcome to our world!'

Up to Speed

It is Tuesday, 2 July 2019, and there's a burst bass-drum skin lying on the footpath at the end of my street, an arc of blood spray inwards towards the centre from the point where the bass drummer's wrist, repeatedly and with great force, met the skin's steel rim. You don't beat the bass drum in Belfast, you blatter it. And carry a spare – or two – for whenever it yields to the laws of physics.

Last night, hundreds of bandsmen and women led Orange Lodges around the streets of east Belfast (sitting MP: Gavin Robinson, DUP) on the annual Somme Memorial parade. I know to call it Somme Memorial parade now, but I had always when I was growing up referred to it as the Mini Twelfth (the 'Wee' Twelfth others called it), a curtain-raiser, no more, for the main event in the Orange calendar, the Twelfth of July. The anniversary of the Battle of the Boyne in 1690. Though in truth the curtain is raised inch by inch, foot by marching foot from sometime in April, and lowered just as gradually until the end of the 'season', on what's known as the Last Saturday in August.*

---

* Strictly speaking, the Last Saturday in August is not Orange, but Black,

One of the main roads out of the city, the Albertbridge Road, just beyond the station where the Dublin train stops, was closed to traffic this evening from half past six. Police erected corrugated iron sheets along the north side of the road where normally a combination of railings and carefully cultivated shrubbery delineate the (nationalist) Short Strand district, where any parade involving the Orange Order is considered a provocation. Elsewhere, including at the end of my street, folding chairs had started to appear on the kerbside even before the roads were closed. On some, the chair owners had set trays of sandwiches covered with cling film. In what would on any other evening at that hour be Urban Clearway, cars were parked with the windows down and the radios on.

The Somme is big in Northern Ireland: part battle, part foundation myth. Of 57,000 British casualties on 1 July 1916 – the costliest day in British military history – 4,900, or approaching one in ten, were serving with the 36th Ulster Division, drawn from a region with something more like one in thirty-five of the United Kingdom population. Over 2,000 of these died, more than 300 from the city of Belfast. (The city's losses rise to 375 when soldiers serving with other regiments are added in.) All this was occurring less than ten weeks after Irish Volunteers, supported by the Irish Citizen's Army, and taking advantage of the war in France

---

being the major parading day of the Royal Black Institution, formed in 1797, a couple of years after the Orange Order. Since membership of the former is only open to members of the latter, black here can be thought of as simply a deeper shade of orange.

('England's difficulty, Ireland's opportunity'), occupied buildings across Dublin in the doomed (at least in the moment) Easter Rising.

Many – if not the majority – of those going over the top at the Somme had themselves been members of the Ulster Volunteer Force (the UVF, on which the Irish Volunteers were modelled).* They had been contemplating a rebellion of their own against a proposed Home Rule Bill ('Home Rule, Rome Rule', was their slogan), which they put aside to serve the country they had been prepared to take up arms against.

About five or six miles further east of my street on Tuesday, 2 July, the five-star Culloden Estate and Spa (motto *foi est tout*: faith is all) is playing host to Jeremy Hunt and Boris Johnson, the two remaining runners in the Tory leadership race, in town for a hustings debate before an audience of five hundred Northern Irish Conservatives. Or maybe that sentence should read: before an audience of Northern Ireland's five hundred Conservatives. Or maybe (again) *ostensibly for* an audience of Northern Ireland's Conservatives. Really, they are both coming to talk to the Democratic Unionist Party.

Those negotiations Theresa May entered into in the wake of the 2017 election produced a Draft Withdrawal Agreement that included a protocol to ensure that the land border between Northern Ireland and the Republic of Ireland remained open,

---

* To this day, the IRA refers to its members as Volunteers – Óglaigh in Irish. Óglaigh Na hÉireann is at one and the same time the name of choice of the Provisional IRA, the official name of the Republic of Ireland's standing army (it grew out of an earlier version of the IRA) and the name of a recently formed 'dissident' republican group.

without customs or police checks, no matter what the terms of the UK's departure from the EU: the 'backstop'.

(How touching now to look at the word dozing in my 2007 Oxford English Dictionary between 'backstitch' and 'backstory' – a little nod, next to it, towards its English sporting equivalent, the long-stop – all unaware of the prominence it was about to achieve.)

The backstop, requiring continued regulatory alignment between the whole of the UK and the EU, with Northern Ireland alone cleaving to certain principles of the single market, proved so unpalatable to Tory Brexiteers – the extreme wing of the Leave campaign – and to the DUP that a further 'instrument' was introduced acknowledging that the measure was 'suboptimal' and that both the EU and the UK did not want to see it come into force: would do everything in their collective powers, in fact, to ensure that it didn't.

And still the Brexiteer objections remained.

After three failed attempts to get the Withdrawal Agreement – with backstop – through the House of Commons, Theresa May revised back the date for the UK leaving the EU by a couple of hundred days and, hard on the heels of that, announced her intention to quit as Prime Minister and Leader of the Conservative Party. The contest began to find her successor.

Two weeks in, I finally understood that the Tory Party leadership contest was actually a Radio 4 comedy panel show in the vein of *I'm Sorry I Haven't a Clue*, whose most famous game, for many years, was 'Mornington Crescent', a game that operated to rules no one but (or possibly including) the contestants understood, and the point of which was to 'arrive' at Mornington Crescent by way of other randomly (though passed off as strategically) named London underground stations. For 'Mornington Crescent' read 'Hard Border', only, instead of *arriving* there, the object of the game is to avoid it altogether, without relying on the word 'backstop'. The one who tells the stupidest, most obvious lie proceeds to the next round. Rory Stewart does surprisingly well to begin with but – alarm bells should have rung when he mentioned he had been reading Seamus Heaney, *The Cure at Troy* of all things, with its oft-quoted line about hope and history rhyming, showing far too much actual interest and knowledge – he comes a cropper when he appears to misunderstand this particular game and talks about how the return of a hard border might *actually* be avoided… Buzzers all round from the other contestants, sympathetic groans from the audience: yes, I'm afraid, Rory, you used the b-s word!

And suddenly I remember my friend Kathleen, a casting agent in New York, who told me a couple of years back about the TV series she was working on, the script of which had not yet been completed at the start of the last day of filming. How I laughed as she related the whole sorry farce of actors all on standby, taxis with their meters running.

This is no way to make television!

I'll tell you something else for nothing, it's no way to leave an economic and political union either. No script, and no idea who the main actors are going to be when it comes to the final act.

So, eleven Tory candidates quickly became ten, became nine, became, at last, the two who have fetched up, this second evening of July, at the Culloden Hotel. The renegotiated withdrawal date of 31 October is 121 days away and still the border in Ireland and the backstop are the great unanswered questions, the issues on which Brexit will stand or fall. (I use 'the border in Ireland' there and not the 'Irish Border' taking my lead from comedian Dara Ó Briain. The 'Irish border', he says, is the beach.*)

And guess what?

The questions are still left unanswered (unless you think saying 'the backstop must change or go' for the nine hundredth time, or muttering about alternative arrangements, is an answer†), at least by Boris Johnson and Jeremy Hunt, as Wednesday, 3 July dawns and 121 becomes 120 days to go and I finally pick up the burst bass-drum skin from the footpath at the end of my street and look for a bin big enough to put it in.

I appreciate that, for some readers, a lot of this will not be new. And then again, others will be like Karen Bradley, the former Secretary of State for this part of the UK, who was blissfully unaware of certain fundamentals of life here. Say, that people

---

* Mind you, one of the most consistently funny critiques of the whole Brexit project is the Irish Border twitter page (@BorderIrish), written in the 'person' of the border itself: 'I am the border between Ireland and Northern Ireland. I'm seamless & frictionless already, thanks. Bit scared of physical infrastructure…' 'I'm getting addicted to messing things up,' reads one tweet. 'I'm going to see what I wreck next after Brexit.' I think this book might already have got it in the neck from them too. If you are reading this and the UK has yet to leave the EU, @BorderIrish called it right.

† Alternative Arrangements is the name of a florist's in Ramsbottom, Lancashire. Maybe Boris Johnson is thinking of landscaping the border (shades of his failed London Garden Bridge). Sagacious? Perhaps not. Herbaceous? Totally.

in Northern Ireland have historically had a tendency to vote along religious lines, or that quite a large percentage of the population consider at least some of the killings for which the police and army were responsible in the course of our Troubles (Bloody Sunday, Ballymurphy, Secretary of State?) to be crimes.

I list among my hobbies emailing eBay sellers to explain that there is no such thing as the 'Mainland UK', no such thing as the UK indeed without Northern Ireland, that postage rates to Belfast are identical to postage rates to Belmarsh, Belshill and Benllech, and that actually they *can* deliver their excellent used-condition shoes to me without surcharge. Though the misconception is not peculiar to eBay sellers. I remember a frantic phone call from my first London publishing house, in the late 1980s, asking me if they needed 'special stamps' to send me proofs of my novel.

(On the phone this summer to an Apple Tech guy – Australian – trying to find me an appointment with a Genius. 'Does *North Ireland* fall under the UK?' he asks. Fall under? Well, when you put it like that...)

Northern Ireland is an administrative region of the UK. Not a country (though it competes as one in FIFA and UEFA competitions and in the Commonwealth Games), still less a province: Ulster, one of the four provinces on the island of Ireland, has nine counties, including Cavan, Donegal and Monaghan, which are in the Republic of Ireland. Northern Ireland, shorn of those three, has six.

At primary school we were taught FAT LAD as a mnemonic: Fermanagh, Antrim, Tyrone, Londonderry, Armagh, Down. I used it as the title of my second novel, which immediately identified me to some people as Protestant by upbringing: a Catholic would not recognize or countenance the L. County Derry, they would say, rather than Londonderry (a few objectors stop their cars on roads heading to the northwest to adjust the signage accordingly), giving you FAT DAD, or indeed DAFT AD... for how to settle one constitutional crisis by storing up another. The Government of Ireland Act of 1920, which created the land border on the island, was ushered in at the height of the first of the twentieth century's Troubles – all-island in this instance – which had picked up where it had left off before the First World War: nationalists set on Home Rule (as a minimum now) and unionists, concentrated in the northeast, determined to resist inclusion in what they feared would be a notably Catholic state.

Reading again about the negotiations – machinations – leading up to Partition, you can't help but hear echoes of the current Brexit wheezes, a lot of leaving but not really leaving, remaining but not really remaining, time-bound opt-outs...* (The quip made about one ardent Partitionist – 'he never knows what he wants but is always intriguing to get it' – could have come straight from the mouth of Donald Tusk.)

---

* There was a short period of time, in December 1922, when Northern Ireland was neither one thing nor the other, having had to opt out of the Irish Free State before it could opt back into the Union. I imagine successive UK prime ministers lying awake at night regretting that the interregnum was so brief.

From 1920 to 1972 we had our own parliament, at Stormont, which, by virtue of the very fact that one (predominantly Catholic) third of Ulster had been excluded from Northern Ireland (those counties weren't left out just for the sake of an acronym), was guaranteed to return a Unionist government. Time after time after time. Catholics were entitled to vote in these and in Westminster elections. As many as three in ten, though, along with a smaller number of Protestants,* were excluded from elections to local councils – where crucial decisions about public housing allocations were made – by virtue of the property requirement, which conversely (perversely) gave some wealthy Protestants several votes. The demand of the Northern Ireland Civil Rights Association (NICRA) for 'One Man One Vote' in the late 1960s therefore looked in two directions: giving to those who had none and taking from those who had too many.†

Worse still was the manipulation of electoral ward boundaries – 'gerrymandering' – which ensured that even where there was a Catholic majority, Protestants still retained control of most councils. NICRA was formed in January 1967, though agitation around housing had been building since 1964. Extreme unionists dismissed it as a front for communists and republicans. The writer Anne Devlin, who 'bunked off' school

* A BBC *Tonight* report puts the figure for Protestants at 15 per cent and dramatized the difference between Westminster and local elections by showing a family of seven adults outside their house: all are eligible to vote in general elections, but – five suddenly disappear – only two in local.
† The Stormont government had not brought in this property requirement, it had just not got rid of it, as the rest of the UK had in its local elections immediately after the Second World War.

to go on Civil Rights marches, says they weren't all about 'Civil Rights for Catholics': '… this was our generation in a show of strength. Of course there were communists and republicans – why not? It's a democracy.'[1]

The Civil Rights campaign gathered force throughout 1968 and into 1969, and at every stage was met with ever-greater resistance from those extreme unionists (including some in uniform), whose anger only increased when the more liberal (very small 'l') government of Captain Terence O'Neill attempted to introduce a measure of reform.

Then, in August 1969, the lid came off. A parade by the Apprentice Boys in Derry in the middle of that month led to an outbreak of rioting in the Catholic Bogside, which stretched into a second and then a third day. (As I was writing this, I heard Carmel McCafferty interviewed on a Radio Ulster programme to mark the fiftieth anniversary of this 'Battle of the Bogside'[2] about the feeling of freedom from throwing her first stone – not necessarily, as it may have looked, at the 'Orangemen' and the police: 'I was throwing it at my boss, who was paying me – I was twenty-one at the time – three pounds a week.')

Violence spread from Derry to Belfast, where the sectarian geography of the city – Catholics and Protestants in some cases living at opposite ends of the same street – meant that it was even nastier, and very quickly bloodier too. British troops were introduced to one city after the other and what was intended as a solution to the problem became a very large part of the problem itself. And the pattern was established for the next quarter of a century.

Several attempts were made to establish power-sharing governments, most notably in 1974 following the Sunningdale Agreement, but all were opposed or thwarted, by republicans and loyalists alike, until the 1998 Belfast – aka Good Friday – Agreement: 'Sunningdale for Slow Learners', as Seamus Mallon, the inaugural Deputy First Minister of our Legislative Assembly, dubbed it.

The Agreement consists of three strands (or Three Strands, to show that they aren't just any old strands): Strand One, the Assembly and ruling Executive; Strand Two, North–South bodies; and Strand Three, their East–West equivalents. All three to be interlocking and interdependent.

The Executive is headed by a First and Deputy First Minister. The Deputy First Minister is actually Joint First Minister: like love and marriage you can't have one without the other.* The office, though officially now the Executive Office, is still referred to by most people, in one breath, as OFMdFM (in Northern Ireland, even the use of the lower-case 'd' is significant and probably the result of a week's negotiation): the Office of First and deputy First Minister.

Uniquely among the constituent parts of the UK, there is no requirement for Members of our Legislative Assembly (MLAs) to take an oath of allegiance to the Queen. The existence – persistence – of the oath at Westminster is central to the refusal of the seven MPs from Sinn Féin to take their

---

* I refer of course to the gospel of Sammy Cahn, whose 'Love and Marriage' lyric runs on, 'Try, try, try to separate them, it's an illusion'. You could drop that straight into the Good Friday Agreement.

seats there, although, you will more often hear that policy of abstention spoken of in terms of jurisdiction: the party refuses to recognize the UK parliament's right to a say in the affairs of any part of Ireland, which remains in their eyes one nation, indivisible (though a man Gerry Adams once referred to as a 'good' republican, Thomas 'Slab' Murphy, former IRA Chief of Staff, serial smuggler and convicted tax evader, could take cognizance of the fact that in matters of revenue in regard to fuel and pigs, the nation is currently – if scarcely visibly – divided and profits from the translation of said goods, backwards and forwards, forwards and backwards, from one jurisdiction to the other).

Sinn Féin likewise, for most of the twentieth century, refused to give credence to the Dublin government – the 'Free State' government as they would have it, using the name coined by the Government of Ireland Act that brought about Partition. They looked back for their authority to the last pre-Partition election, in 1918: a Sinn Féin landslide everywhere but the northeast where the constituencies won by the Irish Unionists (as they still were) formed a shape remarkably similar to today's Northern Ireland.

Earlier this year, a mural went up in Divis Street: '1919 [the date that the first Dáil met] to 2019. This is our mandate. This is our revolution.' Which puts our Brexiteers' fetishization of a referendum held a mere three years ago into perspective.

The party ended its abstention from the Dáil in 1986, though only after an extraordinary (in more senses than one) meeting of the IRA's General Army Council. Not that there was ever any formal connection between Sinn Féin and that mysterious and illegal body. No, there wasn't. No, really. Gerry Adams has spent decades denying he was ever a member of the IRA, let alone its ruling Army Council.)

Some other things of note: at time of writing, you cannot get an abortion unless your life is at risk or there is a risk of permanent and serious damage to your mental or physical health. (In the last year for which there are figures, this came to a grand total of sixteen cases, while 1,053 women went to either England or Wales in 2018 – one in five of the non-nationals seeking terminations in both countries. Three in five were from the Republic of Ireland, whose reform of the abortion law came too late to have any effect on the figure.[3]) By the time you are reading this, however, abortion laws might not only be the equal of the rest of the island, and the Kingdom, but, thanks to the intervention of parliament at the beginning of July, legislating on what had hitherto been considered a devolved matter, they might well be more liberal.

The Northern Ireland (Executive Formation and Exercise of Functions) Bill, which allowed this to happen, could yet turn out to be the most important piece of legislation to come before parliament in a generation. (Trust me, for another seventy pages, I will explain.)

Again uniquely on the islands of Britain and Ireland, in Northern Ireland you cannot marry the person you love if they happen to be of the same gender. Again, and for the same reason that the abortion law has been amended, that might have changed by the time you sit down to read this.

*

You can, however – the 2013 Defamation Act not extending to this side of the Irish Sea – come here expressly to be insulted, and sue, even if the perceived slight, or slander, would be (or indeed had already been) thrown out of court elsewhere in the UK. David Miscavige, the Scientology leader, has availed of this on more than one occasion to prevent the screening of *Going Clear: Scientology and the Prison of Belief*, Alex Gibney's 2015 exposé of his church-cum-corporation-cum-total-fucking-scam. (Other corporate, scammy churches are, I need hardly say, available.)

Until as recently as 2008 you could not play association football professionally or semi-professionally on a Sunday. Members of the Free Presbyterian Church picketed the first match after the lifting of the ban, between Glentoran and Bangor (rescheduled after heavy rain the previous day). Reigning champions Linfield still have a never-on-a-Sunday home game rule, and in truth even the opportunities for away games would still be few and far between. Rugby is another no-no, though you can, and always could, play the full range of competitive Gaelic games: football, hurling, camogie, handball and rounders.*

(Gaelic rounders differs from the English version: bigger

---

* When DUP leader Arlene Foster crossed the border to County Monaghan in June 2018 for the Ulster GAA Football Final, between Donegal and her home county of Fermanagh, she recognized that some people (in her own constituency, that is) might be uncomfortable with her being there 'on a Sunday'.

balls, for one thing, and bats, though it says something for the discipline of the Gaelic rounders family that their bats are never mentioned in connection with so-called paramilitary 'punishment' attacks, unlike baseball bats – more numerous than the popularity of the sport would seem to merit – or indeed iron bars, or sticks with nails driven into them. Or – perennial favourite – guns.)

As of summer 2019, you can also officially play the world's oldest golf tournament, the Open, which took place at Royal Portrush across the third weekend of July, the competition's 'first departure from the UK mainland', as the *Guardian* inaccurately styled it, 'since 1951'. The 1951 tournament was also held in Portrush but the final round was played on Friday afternoon. Besides, the Free Presbyterian Church had only been founded a couple of months before. Even if it had been a Sunday they might not have had time to get their act, or their placards, together.

You can order a drink in most bars most weekend nights and many weekday nights after 11 p.m. After midnight, indeed. One of the arguments put forward for extending the licensing hours was that unofficial drinking clubs – shebeens – many of which were run by, or contributed to the coffers of, paramilitary organizations, were serving into the wee small hours. One of the arguments not put forward was that the First World War – when pub opening hours were curtailed throughout the whole of the UK – had ended nearly a century before.

*

Speaking of bars, after years of arguing to the contrary, I am forced to accept that our bank notes – Ulster, Danske, First Trust, Bank of Ireland – are not strictly speaking legal tender in the rest of the UK. (In fact, very, very strictly, they may not even be in Northern Ireland.) They are promissory notes: the banks that issue them have to have Bank of England notes or coin or equivalent Bank of England investment equal to the value of all the notes in circulation at any given time.

(The Provisional IRA did the Bank of England a solid favour by removing 26.5 million Northern – forerunner of Danske – Bank notes from circulation one Sunday night in December 2005, to help, it was said at the time, with its volunteers' 'pension' fund. By buying them villas in Bulgaria, apparently, and – unwisely, given the events of September 2008 – investing in the New York stock exchange.)

To all the English bar staff I rowed with, those 1980s student days when I had received a letter from home with an Ulster or Bank of Ireland fiver in it and beat a path to your various doors, one after the other after the other... Sorry.

Oh, and holidays... Unlike the rest of the UK, where you wait until it's practically autumn before going and sitting for several days in an airport wondering why nobody has told you anything at all about your cancelled flight, people here tend to go away for the days – and if they can manage it, weeks – either side of the Twelfth of July. It's a carry-over from the times when the 'Twelfth Fortnight' was tantamount to an enforced nationwide (sorry: administrative-region-wide) shutdown, or perhaps – for a younger generation – those more recent days when summer parades were the occasions of stand-offs and outbreaks of rioting.

Radio 4's *Today* programme had planned to broadcast from Derry this year on Saturday, 13 July, the weekend before the start of the Open in not-far-distant Portrush. The producers were hoping to interview someone connected to a children's writing charity – Fighting Words Belfast – that I am involved in. Everyone involved in the charity with me was hoping *Today* would be able to interview one of us. Of the six people copied into the email, however, not one was planning to be in Northern Ireland that weekend.

The world's press descends, and those of us who don't march, or watch golf, and can, skedaddle. I skedaddled much farther than I usually do – all the way to Canada, in fact – though I would still have got up at – or stayed up until – three in the morning to do an interview 'down the line'. Just a few weeks before, the Ireland Funds had awarded Fighting Words their prestigious literary prize in memory of Lyra McKee, the journalist murdered in Derry in April by so-called dissident republicans. We were keen, all of us, to express our gratitude – to the Ireland Funds and to Sara Canning, Lyra's partner, who had given the award her blessing – and to talk about the project we hope to be able to start in Derry...

Three days before the planned broadcast, however, *Today* gave up trying to find anyone at all to talk to and decided to come back in the middle of the autumn, when everyone in England was finally back from holiday.

One of the current prime movers of Fighting Words Belfast is Emily DeDakis, who was also involved in setting up a theatre company – Accidental – that has staged, among other things, the very popular *Thelma-and-Louise*-inspired *Michele and Arlene* (O'Neill and Foster, that is, leaders of Sinn Féin and the DUP respectively) by Belfast playwright Rosemary Jenkinson. She is contributing mightily to the conversation here – and to the fun.

Emily grew up in Washington, D.C., and Atlanta, and arrived here, by way of New Orleans, in 2005. She still says, 'Belfast is a particularly challenging place to not be from.'

And that's without taking Brexit into account.

Emily's partner – Tom – is from Wexford. Up to now, he and she have been able to live here due to his EU citizenship. Post-Brexit, her status (rather than his) becomes more complicated. I ran into her on the last Saturday night in June at Belfast Ensemble's *Lunaria*, part of a triple-bill of musical theatre composed by Conor Mitchell, the other two being *The Fall of the House of Usher* and *The Cunt of Queen Catherine*. The last time I saw *The Cunt of Queen Catherine*, which is not a sentence you often write, two and more years ago now, it was presented as *The Moot Virginity of Catherine of Aragon* – Part 1 of 2 Habsburg Tragedies, of which the second was *The Last Confession of Juana the Mad*, Juana being Catherine of Aragon's sister, the first monarch of a united Spain.

The works were begun when the Referendum was first

mooted and were, their writer says, explicitly conceived of as a way – by going back to an earlier moment of schism – to talk about Europe here and now (or there and then). 'In Northern Ireland we felt a possible split could have far-reaching consequences for us – most importantly the border and the peace process.' (Note, Mr Johnson, he thought this even before the Referendum date was set.)

As he said at the time, if we weren't able in future to send a Marks & Spencer's van from Belfast to Dublin without rigorous customs checks, how on earth were we going to bring Danish State Opera here? As it was, he said, theatre in Northern Ireland was so cut off from outside influence it had evolved like a marsupial.

That night – in spring 2017 – was the first time I met people, up from Dublin to catch the show, travelling with their passports in their pockets, in case they got stopped at the border. A few weeks later, another American friend living in Belfast was on the bus down to Dublin when the Guards (*Garda Síochána*) got on and started checking papers. My friend wasn't travelling with any. She never did. The Guards took her off the bus and brought her to Dundalk Garda station while they checked her story out.

Lunaria, Conor Mitchell's new piece, named for the flower commonly known as 'honesty', has three vocalists facing one another on a rudimentary stage, around which sit half a dozen musicians (two violins, cello, piano, clarinet and flute), conducted energetically. Their words are taken from news reports from the past two-and-a-bit years of Northern Ireland affairs, starting with the resignation of Martin McGuinness as Deputy First Minister in January 2017 and ending with the murder of Lyra McKee.

The refrain, 'What is the backstop?', is boiled down and down until only the last word remains – spoken by each performer in turn twenty (or is it more?) times. It – along with others – is projected on a screen behind the performers.

The word Brexit is given its phonetic transcription, which turns out to be the same as the Serbian, and very close to the Ulster Scots – or Ulster English – or Northern Irish English (the jury on the correct term is out), as in one of the best responses I have yet read by a writer from here to the contortions of the political discourse, the poem by Elaine Gaston printed at the start of this book:

We don know yet fthere'll be
a clean Breggsit ra messy Breggsit
nur a hard Breggsit nur a saft Breggsit.
But mnot goin te build a hard boarder.
It'll be a soft boarder, waitn see.
A sorta magic boarder that no-one can see.
We can hay a boarder that isny a boarder.
One tay keep youse in, an everyone else oot.

*

The population of Northern Ireland currently stands at 1.87 million people. I had this figure confirmed for me by the kid with the curly hair and braces on the G1 Glider (Belfast's new purple bendy bus), who was trying to convince his younger brother that he had been one of the first people in the city to ride a Glider when they were introduced in autumn 2018. 'I'll bet at least a couple of million were on it on before you,' his brother said. At which point Curly Hair and Braces pulled out his phone. 'How could they have? A couple is two and, look,' thumbing up a page, 'there's only 1.87 million in the whole of Northern Ireland.'

About one in three live in the Greater Belfast area. The figure for the city itself, though, is still a shade under 300,000* and is – according to a very impatient Irish-American businessman I heard speak at a conference in New York last year – likely to keep 'floundering' around that level until we do something about our rents... lower them, you might think he meant, but, no: Belfast, it seems, is the 'reverse opposite of most reasonable cities' in that the 'lower socio-economic classes live in the centre.'

In the very, very centre, in fact, according to architect Ciaran Mackel, there are only just slightly more people living today than there were in 1750, in the region of 9,000. During the Troubles,† when the inner core of the city was ringed with

---

* I am reminded again as I write that of Belfast novelist Robert McLiam Wilson's assertion that Belfast was basically 'Stoke with guns'.
† An inadequate term, I realize, and as many have pointed out, for what occurred here from the late 1960s on, and cost thousands of people their lives. In its singular form, though, it is the word I remember hearing most often when I was growing up: 'Watch yourself going into town, there was trouble there earlier.'

security gates, the number was substantially lower. In fact, Pat Catney, former owner of the Kitchen Bar, put the number living within the gates during the worst years at six, and three of those were living above the Kitchen.

'It's difficult to entice equity capital into Belfast at £20 a square foot... at £30 it begins to make sense.' This again from the irate businessman 'The reason there has been so much development in the Titanic Quarter' – the largest development project in the city in what used to be the city's, and the world's, largest shipyard (I'll be taking you there soon enough) – 'is that the land is cheap. The challenge now is to get the rents up...' And travel times down: the businessman turned puce when he mentioned the two-hour train journey to Dublin, 102 miles away: 'You should be doing that in less than half that time!'

And, miserably, I find myself agreeing with him, as I suspect might anyone who has found themselves sitting on a train, unexpectedly becalmed somewhere on the Belfast–Dublin rail line, or saying goodbye to friends at 8 o'clock in the evening as they dash to make the last train north. (There are buses after that, but the buses – crucially – don't have toilets, which makes the prospect of sitting for two-and-a-bit hours after a longer night out... daunting.) But that's all the agreement he's getting out of me.

The businessman I heard in New York is not alone. As far back as 2012, the chief executive of Titanic Quarter Limited, David Gavaghan, was telling the Annual Northern Ireland Economic Conference that Belfast needed to double its population to take advantage of the future growth areas of technology, tourism, sport, leisure and energy.

The Irish Congress of Trade Unions, which had not been invited to contribute, picketed the conference, and picketed again the year after, claiming it would be 'used to resurrect the failed economic policies of reckless lending, vulture capitalism and corporate greed', a small reminder that the kind of booming backstop-enabled Belfast some in the business community have in mind might not benefit those people who currently live in the heart of it.

'We should be attracting more people from abroad but also keeping some from leaving and ensuring that those who are away can come back,' Gavaghan said. With which only a churl would argue. This is still a place that people want to leave. Belfast is the only city in the UK with a net loss of working-age people: 57 per cent of school-leavers head south, or cross one or other of the bodies of water that surround us. The figure for school-leavers emigrating from the Republic of Ireland is 6 per cent and from Scotland is 4 per cent. In return, we attract only 4.4 per cent of other people's. It's difficult to see Brexit in any but its gentlest form reversing that.

I am trying to write this book in real time – or as real as these unreal and rumour-filled times get (someone assured me just the other week that the IRA did not decommission their weapons back in 2006, they sent them to northern Spain and now have brought them back again). I am trying very hard to keep up, but the moment will come when I will have to stop, hands on hips, panting, and events carry on past me (oh-oh, here comes Angela Merkel's thirty-day challenge! And, wait – Dominic Grieve, and fuck me, Johnson's only gone and prorogued parliament – oh wait a minute, no he hasn't) to wherever they are headed next, I prefer to think, rather than 'their destination'. Nothing that human beings contrive – no matter how appalling – is final. I cling to the thought that for good or ill, everything is reversible. Apart from the climate – unless we all get our act together pretty damn quick, none of this other stuff is going to matter in fifty or a hundred years' time.

I am sitting, the second Saturday morning in August, writing – in fact I am looking at the passage about Emily DeDakis and about this being a particularly difficult place to not be from – when my home phone rings. A friend of Ali, my wife, who, as it happens, is out. We get to talking about what we are both up to. I tell her I am working on this book. She sighs, from somewhere very deep down. 'I can't stay here if [Brexit] happens,' she says.

Liz, like my wife, who she got to know in Cork, moved to Belfast in the mid-1990s, against the advice of practically everyone she knew down there. Her daughter was born here – cue even more advice from everyone she knew at home to leave, but the ceasefires had just been called. 'I thought, fuck it,' she tells me, 'I'm staying.'

She worked as an artist and as a community arts facilitator in areas suffering high levels of deprivation. So much a part of the place did she feel that when she did briefly move South again, in 2007, she found she couldn't integrate. 'People were whining about not being able to take their second and third holidays. I felt like saying to them, you want to take a trip up to north Belfast. There's nowhere like north Belfast in the

South… No, wait, I passed an abandoned Famine village once in the middle of a bog. That was a bit like it.' After only a few months, she moved back.

And now? 'I've given it my all. I can't become even more cut off,' calling to mind a conversation I had with another friend, a lifelong Belfast resident, straight after the Referendum. 'I was only able to stay here all these years because I thought I was part of something bigger. I don't want to be living in the outpost of somebody else's kingdom.'

'It's a cultural backwater,' Liz says, 'and it's getting worse… I need to go somewhere where I feel I have a value. Two things have been preoccupying me the past few years, sex and death. They just have a better approach to both in the South. The people up here are still thinking we're all numpties down there, and people down there are still saying, oh, but your health service is so much better… I'm thinking, you are divided by nothing and you have no clue about one another. Imagine what it's going to be like if all this goes ahead.

'I'm not a particular fan of either [the Irish Taoiseach] Leo Varadkar or [his Tánaiste] Simon Coveney, but they're genuine, and the way they're being talked to, like Johnny Irelander… It's made me ill, the whole thing.'

She looks back with regret to that 2017 snap election, not because it set the tone for Brexit but because it was so damaging for Northern Ireland, hardening the attitudes of voters here – '[it] destroyed the first chance we had had to break out of that Orange and Green mindset,' is how she puts it. Just before she rings off, she tells me she is seeking solace in Seneca. 'It's good to go back and remind yourself it was ever thus.'

Perhaps she has in mind the lines from *Moral Letters to Lucilius* (Letter 71, 'On the supreme good'): 'Our plans miscarry because they have no aim. When a man does not know what harbour he is making for, no wind is the right wind.'

Later that same day, I am on the top deck of a bus out of town, headed east. (Not a Glider. If you are on the top deck of a Glider reading this, I want you to listen to me very, very carefully… Jump! *There is no top deck on the Glider!*) Two men – I guess in their mid-sixties – meet in the double seat across the aisle from me. They fall to discussing the price of pints – £3.40 in this club, £3.20 in that, a fiver and more, now, in some of the bars down the town ('wild,' one of them says) – breaking off as we come over the Albert Bridge for a brief political discussion.

'What do you reckon to Johnson?' the man in the window seat asks.

His friend draws his head back to give him the full benefit of his contempt: 'If there's one thing I hate in life, it's stupidity… Dickhead.'

And then they're back to parsing the price of pints in points east of the Albert Bridge.

Everybody has an angle, I suppose, so here is mine. I grew up in a predominantly Protestant housing estate, in the south of the city. In 1971, Protestants became even more predominant after several Catholic families were intimidated out of their homes and other families moved in who had fled intimidation

elsewhere. My father described himself as British (the pass-
port), my mother as Irish (the island). I built bonfires for the
Eleventh of July. I walked once on the Twelfth, when I was
thirteen, helping to carry the banner (well, helping to hold
the strings that kept the banner that other, bigger people
carried from flapping) of a friend's dad's lodge. In my later
teens I stopped with the bonfires and the parades – went
out of my way, in fact, to avoid them. When I went across
the water to university, in the early 1980s, I hung about with
people who were in the Socialist Workers' Student Society
– SWSS, pronounced Swizz. (I attended meetings but never
actually joined, not out of scrupulousness or squeamishness.
If I remember right, I drank the money I had set aside to pay
the subscription.) A good many of the Swizzers were also in
the Troops Out Movement. I would go to parties in student
houses with posters on the walls saying things like 'IRA Calls
the Shots'.

I read with interest, and with every intention of supporting,
a mid-1980s Sinn Féin European election manifesto that left me
instead sitting open-mouthed at its suggestion that membership of the (then) EEC was diluting Irish identity and culture. I
couldn't see where I fitted into the identity and culture they were
invoking either. (Reading that manifesto again now – thank you,
Internet – I wonder whether the UK's Leave campaign might
not have nicked a few lines from it.)

Not long after that, in November 1985, came the Anglo-
Irish Accord: 'diktat' in the view of its Unionist opponents,
and believe me, no one can get more dik – or tat – into diktat
than an irate Ulster Presbyterian preacher. To quote the poet

W. R. Rogers, who himself had served his time in the pulpit, 'I am Ulster, my people an abrupt people/Who like the spiky consonants in speech.'

The Accord gave the Dublin government a limited consultative role in Northern Ireland's affairs. Tens of thousands of Protestants took to the streets of Belfast, massing at the City Hall to hear Ian Paisley utter his famous 'Never! Never! Never!'* Some portion of them peeled off from the main body and looted a sports shop and pelted the police with golf balls. Watching all this on TV with my English friends, I heard that phrase for the first time: 'Who the fuck are these people?' I thought I probably knew quite a number of them by name. I wrote a novel while still living in England, set in a (predominantly Protestant) Belfast housing estate – complete with bonfire – the year the Troubles began. I moved back to Belfast to write another novel set in the present day (the summer, that is, of 1990, now almost as distant in the rear-view mirror as my birth was when I started it). I met a lot of people here who were trying to imagine their way beyond the binary. Some of the conversations they were having – about embracing multiple identities within the self and the body politic, for instance – seemed to me to be of moment to more

---

* I am perhaps presuming a touch too much by not inserting 'mostly' or 'almost exclusively' between 'tens of thousands' and 'Protestants'. Aodán Mac Póilin in one of the essays in his wonderful, posthumously published collection, *Our Tangled Speech*, quotes a 2008 'Northern Ireland Life and Times' survey that puts the proportion of Catholics identifying as unionist at 1 per cent, although as Aodán, and the survey, goes on to say, there is a little more to identity than that.

than just Northern Ireland. Here were conversations, I thought, that the rest of these islands could usefully be having, with and between themselves. It was a very exciting place to be.

And that was before the ceasefires.

So, this is the place where – after another couple of years of toing and froing to England – I decided in those still pre-ceasefire days of the early 1990s to… settle. (There's another word that has been co-opted of late, as in, 'EU citizens are "encouraged" to apply for "settled status" ahead of 31 October.' And against, by the way, guarantees made by Theresa May that EU citizens who had, as she said, 'built their lives in the UK' would automatically have their rights protected.)

I voted Yes to the Good Friday Agreement in 1998, along with 676,965 (71.12 per cent) of my fellow Northern Irish citizens, Remain in 2016, along with 789,878 of them (55.8 per cent). If presented with the same two choices again, I would vote the same way but I would reserve, even so, the right to complain when things look fucked up.

Speaking of which…

Up on the Hill

Stormont (1)

The complete works of the Northern Ireland Assembly
since January 2017:

*(After Len Shackleton's 'The Average Director's
Knowledge of Football')*

DUP

On Wednesday, 31 July, Boris Johnson is back in Belfast (no Jeremy Hunt now*) as leader of the Conservative Party, Prime Minister of Great Britain and Northern Ireland, First Lord of the Treasury and self-appointed Minister for the Union, for talks with the five main parties here: in alphabetical order, Alliance, the Democratic Unionist Party, Sinn Féin, the Social Democratic and Labour Party (SDLP) and Ulster Unionist Party (UUP). On the agenda, not Brexit, the PM–MU says, but the restoration of the Stormont Assembly/power-sharing government, suspended since January 2017, making us – at rapidly approaching 1,000 days and at a moment when you might have thought we could do with some informed local decision-making – the holders of the world record for the longest time without a government.

---

* This despite Jeremy's offering to make the DUP part of his Withdrawal Agreement renegotiating team, borrowing, if I may say, one of my ideas from as soon as the Referendum result was known. My reckoning was if they could help string out our peace process for twenty-five years it might be a quarter of a century before anything definitive happened with Brexit.

The parties have been 'locked in talks' as they say (inaccurately) since the start of May, shamed into them by the public outrage at the murder of Lyra McKee. As with all previous negotiations since January 2017, though, momentum has been lost and the 'never again' horror of the moment submerged in the tit-for-tat squabbles of an increasingly fractious summer. The Prime Minister is determined, he says, to give all of the parties a fair and equal hearing, as indeed he is obliged to under the terms of the Good Friday Agreement.

So, of course, he began his trip last night with a private dinner in the company of Arlene Foster, Sir Jeffrey Donaldson and other senior members of the DUP, with whom his government is renegotiating the confidence and supply arrangement. He knows them all well. He spoke at their annual party conference last year while out of office, conducting his campaign against Theresa May from the back benches. At the conference, he played them all his Brexit Won't Affect Us hits, including the construction of a bridge to Scotland (which could eventually – cunning indeed – give Northern Ireland a customs barrier with *two* countries still in the EU, since that is where Scotland wishes to be) and invoked Van Morrison in urging his audience that it was time we moved from the dark end of the street to the bright side of the road.

'I like your style,' he had told the delegates ('Us?' I can imagine them thinking, sitting up a little straighter – *even* straighter – in their seats, '*Style?*') before going off on some bizarre riff about 'personal recreational watercraft' ('a Northern Irish pedalo or paddleboard'), intended to illustrate the point that the EU was hostile to innovation and competition.

I was reminded, listening to him, of one of those headlines from the morning after the 2017 General Election: 'Coalition of Crackpots'. The DUP, it meant. But, seriously, pedalos and paddleboards...?

And I am reminded now – seeing the footage of the prime ministerial motorcade arrive at Stormont, this final day of July, the eight-hundred-and-ninety-whateverth since the Assembly was suspended – of the night when this whole power-sharing enterprise began to take shape.

On Friday, 10 April 1998, it snowed. The Northern Irish political parties who had been in intensive negotiations for the previous several weeks (we didn't know then that this was setting the pattern), in negotiations of one form or another for a couple of years, with each other, with the British and Irish governments, and with the United States' government's special envoy, Senator George Mitchell, finally reached an agreement – overdue, as agreements tend to be here (an absolute deadline had been set of midnight on 9 April), but all the more euphonious and felicitous for the overrun: Good Friday instead of Maundy Thursday, or Holy Thursday, or Thursday of Mysteries.

Cameras were admitted, a great many cameras. The parties and the governments and the special envoy, at tables arranged in an open-sided square. The DUP were not there. The party had absented itself from the talks the previous September in protest at the inclusion of Sinn Féin, just six weeks after the resumption of the IRA's ceasefire. Chances are if you remember any ceasefire, it will be the first IRA ceasefire – 31 August 1994 – and after that, possibly, the Loyalist ceasefire of 13 October that same year. It was, however, the second IRA ceasefire of 20 July 1997 – following bombs in Canary Wharf (two dead) and Manchester and several murders at home – that paved the way for the final talks process. Violence didn't end completely – Sinn Féin was suspended from talks on two more occasions in response to further IRA murders – but the suspensions got shorter as the outlines of a deal came into view.[1]

Now on the night of Friday, 10 April, the DUP were – literally – outside the tent as the world's press crowded in to talk to the signatories of the Agreement. This was the pre-personal computer era.* 'You tube' was still a thing you shouted at a friend who had just poured a drink down his front (well, it was here). Things happened and if you weren't alert enough to hit record on your VHS, that was the moment gone, so I don't know how reliable this memory is but in my head I hear the supporters of two of the smaller Unionist parties – the PUP (close to the illegal paramilitary UVF) and the UDP (an emanation of the paramilitary UDA) – singing, 'Cheerio, cheerio, cheerio…'

(Once, in my early thirties, I narrated to my Mum the full story of the night our family car got stopped coming through the centre of town by members of the Parachute Regiment.

---

* Pre-mobile phone too. One BBC journalist who had covered the many, many months of talks since the process began told me that, when the mid-night deadline passed, he went on an Easter break with his family. His bosses tried – and failed – to discover which west coast of Scotland hotel he was in to tell him to get back.

They lined us up against the front of Marks & Spencer and took the car apart looking for guns. I was ten at the time. My mum was amazed at my recall. 'Except,' she said, 'they weren't Paras, they were Military Police, and it wasn't Marks & Spencer either, it was the Grand Central Hotel.' Make of that what you will.)

Footage does survive of a rival press conference that the DUP held on their own that Friday. Their leader, the Revd Dr Ian Paisley (he had recently celebrated his seventy-second birthday), holds up what appears to be a transcript of the Agreement that had just been reached. Paisley looks as though he is winding up to one of his famous rants. Almost before he can speak, though, a shout rings out from somewhere behind the cameras: 'The Grand Old Duke of York!' And for a moment in the laughter that follows, he looks (I freeze the picture) old and lost and confused.

I honestly thought that night that that was it, the DUP were gone, consigned to history.

A word – while I've paused – on the U's of Northern Ireland politics. Whatever isn't 'Unionist' is likely to be 'Ulster', with here and there a 'United' for variation or intensification, or in the case of the UUUP, all three. (I refer you to *Fry's English Delight* for the correct order. In English, says Mark Forsyth, author of *The Elements of Style*, adjectives are arranged by opinion, size, age, shape, colour, origin, material and, finally, purpose.)

Most of them have been short-lived – the UUUP lasted less than ten years (1975–84) – and almost all of them have (like almost all Protestant churches – of Protestantism, indeed) been the product of schism. The UUUP had emerged from the VUPP (Vanguard Unionist Progressive Party, 1972–78). A later party, the UKUP – United and Unionist – split when four of its five elected representatives formed the NIUP (the NI is the best clue that the U here is not Ulster), leaving the party's founder to soldier on alone for a couple more years, anticipating the advent of the (still current) TUV – Traditional Unionist Voice – which is probably best described as the Northern Irish spelling of 'Jim Allister', supporter of evangelical creationist lobby groups and a man who could start a fight in an empty room (welcome to the TUV annual party conference).

The Daddy of them all (alas, the male term still seems appropriate) is the UUP – the Ulster Unionist Party – which has on occasion and somewhat confusingly gone by the acronym O (for Official) UP.

The UUP grew out of the nineteenth-century Irish Unionist Alliance and was, from its formation in 1905 through to 1972, essentially an offshore wing of the British Conservative Party (Conservative *and Unionist*, to give it its full title). Although it has at various times worked closely with it, the DUP was formed essentially in opposition to the UUP.* Its support for

---

* The most notorious instance of DUP–UUP 'cooperation' came in July 1995, after an Orange march had been forced down the nationalist Garvaghy Road in Portadown, against its residents' wishes: as they arrived at their destination party leaders Ian Paisley and David Trimble, both wearing their collarettes ('sash' is almost always a misnomer), took one another's hands in what looked very much like a victory 'jig'. To that summer, I date my own skedaddling.

the Conservative Party likewise has never been a given... more a bought. After the 2010 election, in fact, in the turmoil before the Conservative–Liberal Democrat pact was sealed, Labour had discussions with the DUP about a possible coalition, which puts a slightly different complexion on some of the outrage that came from the liberal left seven years later.

(Here's a question, hypothetical I know, but if a Labour government supported by the DUP had prevented the worst ravages of the austerity regime ushered in by the other pairing, would you have taken it? And would we have ended up with a referendum on EU membership at all?)

The formation of the Democratic Unionist Party was announced by Ian Paisley on 30 September 1971 outside the ruin of the Four Step Inn on the (Protestant) Shankill Road, bombed the night before, with the loss of two lives, by the Provisional IRA.

Paisley already had a considerable profile. He was the anti-Zelig: whatever the occasion – baby-step talks between Northern Irish and Southern Irish premiers (he threw snowballs), ecumenical church initiatives (he flew into London specially on New Year's Day 1969 to protest against the Catholic Cardinal Heenan preaching in St Paul's Cathedral as part of a Week of Prayer for Christian Unity) – he was always there, and always visible, and audibly protesting, and always unmistakably himself.

So identified was he with protest in the 1960s that the catch-all term for what now would be called loyalists, hard-line unionists, was simply 'Paisleyites'. Ordained by his own father (a Baptist minister), he set up his Free Presbyterian Church of Ulster while still in his twenties, and within fifteen years had established a vast Belfast branch on a prosperous section of the Ravenhill Road in east Belfast. (It seemed vast at the time but evangelical Protestant churches have gone on getting vaster in the half-century since: the Metropolitan Tabernacle in north Belfast is so big it nearly qualifies for its own MP.)

In 1964 he had led a protest up Divis Street, which eventually becomes the Falls Road, to protest at the flying of an Irish flag in the window of a republican election candidate's window. When the police tried to remove it, rioting broke out. In 1966 – the same year he did (brief) jail time rather than pay a fine for unlawful assembly (he had been on his way to picket the General Assembly of the Presbyterian Church in Ireland for not being Presbyterian enough, most likely) – he was awarded an honorary doctorate by the Bob Jones University, South Carolina, a Christian fundamentalist college whose founder had been exercised by the spread of evolution-teaching and which at that point in its history still did not admit black students.

Prior to the formation of the DUP, Paisley had led the Protestant Unionist Party (his wife, Eileen Paisley, was one of its first elected representatives), so named presumably to avoid confusion with the so-small-as-to-have-slipped-out-of-the-annals-entirely Catholic Unionist Party and not to be confused either with the later *Progressive* Unionist Party; and before that, in the mid-1960s, he fronted the Ulster Constitution Defence Committee, alongside which an organization called the Ulster Protestant Volunteers (UPV) had been formed. You have to possess ears of cloth in Northern Ireland not to be aware of how that word 'Volunteers' will be heard by other people's.

The UPV adopted the same motto – For God and Ulster – as the UVF, which was also revived around this time: 1966 being the fiftieth anniversary of both the Battle of the Somme and the Easter Rising. Even some of the members appeared to be confused as to which was which. One close associate of Paisley, and co-founder of the UPV, Noel Doherty, was later jailed for explosives offences. That World Cup summer, the UVF carried out sectarian attacks in and around the Shankill Road, culminating in the murder of a young barman, Peter Ward, and attempted murder of three of his colleagues from the International Hotel as they left another bar where they had been having an after-work drink. One of those convicted for those shootings famously said, 'I am sorry I ever heard tell of that man Paisley or decided to follow him.'

Paisley said none of it had anything to do with him.*

Even so, the DUP, like the Ulster Constitutional Defence Committee and the Protestant Unionist Party, has down the years had its share of flirtations with paramilitaries. That is if your definition of flirtation extends to taking off all your clothes, getting under the covers together and, well, it's dark, nobody else can see...

* A documentary being trailed as I finish this book claims that not only had it something to do with him, but that Paisley supplied money to the UVF for bomb attacks on reservoirs and water pipelines in 1969.

An outfit named Third Force was formed in April 1981 and was styled as a 'defensive militia', although given that that other self-styled defence combo the UDA – Ulster *Defence* Association – had been responsible for scores of murders by then, the adjective was hardly a guarantee of peaceful defensive intent. True, the Third Force's activities amounted in the end to a handful of hilltop rallies addressed by Paisley in the course of which firearms certificates were waved in the air (hence the 'Grand Old Duke of York' jibe), but the mere fact of mobilizing hundreds of men – Paisley claimed as many as 20,000 – could not help but appear sinister.

Ulster Resistance, formed in 1986 in opposition to the Anglo-Irish Accord, went a step further in encouraging its members in the wearing of red berets. One of the keenest beret-wearers was Peter Robinson, at the time the DUP's deputy leader, who led a group of a couple of hundred across the border to the village of Clontibret (a few of them had chosen hoods and balaclavas for the occasion instead of their normal headgear), where they beat up a couple of Guards, smashed a window or two and painted the words 'Ulster has Awakened' on the Garda station wall.

When, a couple of years later, police uncovered arms related to Ulster Resistance in County Armagh, the DUP claimed that it no longer had any connection with the movement, just as their party leader had claimed back in 1966 with those Ulster Protestant Volunteers…

I left Paisley paused back there at the press conference, holding up his copy of the Agreement…

Go again.

The DUP campaigned vigorously and vociferously – almost Biblically – against the endorsement of the Agreement in the simultaneous North–South Referendum called for May 1998: 'The so-called Agreement is a devilishly devised transitional arrangement engineered to progressively convey Ulster, through all-Ireland functioning, into a united Ireland...' (Peter Robinson, from DUP 'It's Right to Say NO' campaign literature. As a little counterweight to all the talk of devilishness, the 'O' of 'NO' has a little Union Jack heart at the centre.)

They were helped in their analysis, then and afterwards, by Sinn Féin, who talked up the Agreement to their supporters in precisely the same staging-post-to-unification terms that the DUP used to put the fear of God into theirs, and who have at times seemed more interested in building the party in the South, with a view to getting into government there, than in ensuring that there was a proper functioning government in the North.

Paisley in his appeal to voters gives the party an extra U for emphasis: the *Ulster* Democratic Unionist Party. 'I am saying to [UUP Leader] Mr Trimble, do what you like, say what you like, take any bribe they can give you... the people of Northern Ireland at the Referendum – provided we can see it will not be jigged – will totally and absolutely reject you and what you are attempting to do.'

In fact, 71.12 per cent of the electorate voted in favour. (The 'yes' figure in the South was even higher: 94.46 per cent.) The DUP, even so, claimed victory, Paisley leaving the count centre declaring, 'We won the majority of the *Protestant* vote!'

Unfortunately, this kind of (ac)counting carries weight in Northern Ireland. In 2019, Alastair Campbell, Downing Street Press Secretary at the time of the Good Friday Agreement, made a distinction between today's – dissident – Republicans and the previous generation's. Even at the height of the Troubles, he said, Sinn Féin was getting 30 per cent of the Catholic vote. Yes, but what that figure meant was that even at the height of the Troubles, seven out of ten of the people the IRA claimed to be fighting for rejected their political representatives at the polls.

After five years of what one prominent ex-member calls 'opposition from within', criticizing First Minister David Trimble's UUP at every turn, the DUP was topping the poll in an Assembly election for the first time in its history. The DUP's ranks had by now been swelled by defectors from the UUP unhappy at the outworkings of the Good Friday Agreement. These included some of the most able of the younger generation of UUPers: Jeffrey Donaldson, who had walked out of the Good Friday negotiations at the eleventh hour – which is to say somewhere around 5:15 p.m. – over the failure to secure IRA decommissioning, and future party leader Arlene Foster.

Another to defect was Jonathan Bell, who had far less of a profile outside Northern Ireland and not that much even inside, but whose revelations late in 2016 about the mismanagement (or worse) of the Renewable Heating Incentive (RHI) scheme triggered the chain of events that ended with the Assembly being suspended.

★

The DUP's emergence as the dominant unionist party coincided with Sinn Féin overtaking the SDLP as the main party of Northern nationalism, which in turn heralded (if you can herald something that took four more years to arrive) the second and even more surprising stage of power-sharing, but only after a substantial revisitation of the Good Friday Agreement, the final stages of which took place in the Scottish town of St Andrews in autumn 2006 and produced a new set of principles – the St Andrews Agreement. (At least we know they didn't spend too much of their negotiating time on the name.) St Andrews, crowed the DUP, was 'immeasurably better than the lousy deal negotiated by the UUP in 1998' in that it 'forced republicans, kicking and screaming, down the road of ending paramilitary and criminal activity' and required them to 'openly support the police', as well as the courts and the judicial system, and made all 'North–Southery' accountable to Northern Ireland's representatives.

Paisley later claimed that the only reason he agreed at St Andrews to enter into government with Sinn Féin was the threat otherwise of even greater involvement by the Irish government than the Good Friday Agreement provided for. (It is often said that every generation of unionists finds itself faced with a worse deal than was on offer last time around.) For many, though, it appeared as if the offer of becoming nominal leader of Northern Ireland had proved irresistible. Certainly, his transformation once in the post of First Minister suggested a man finally at ease with himself. At ease too with his partner in government, Deputy First Minister Martin McGuinness, former IRA Chief of Staff, earning them the nickname of the 'Chuckle

Brothers'* much to the alarm of colleagues within the DUP, and his own Free Presbyterian Church, from which he was effectively removed as Moderator after fifty-seven unbroken years in January 2008. A month later he was confronted by – or himself sought a meeting with, depending on who you believe – Nigel Dodds, leader of the party at Westminster, and Peter Robinson, deputy leader of the party at Stormont, who made it clear to him that he had lost the confidence of DUP MPs and MLAs. Robinson duly took over as First Minister but had been in post little more than eighteen months when he too had to stand aside, temporarily, when details emerged of his wife – and fellow DUP politician – Iris Robinson's affair with a teenager, Kirk McCambley, for whom it was alleged she (and her husband) had secured business contracts.

In 2010, in the first election since those allegations, Robinson lost his Belfast (East) parliamentary seat to the Alliance Party, which has traditionally stood on a non-sectarian platform, and whose candidate Naomi Long had grown up in east Belfast, in a working-class neighbourhood close to the Harland & Wolff shipyard.

The DUP went into overdrive. The party – aided and abetted in this case by the UUP – lit on a motion tabled at Belfast City Council and carried with Alliance Party support to restrict the flying of the Union Flag from the City Hall to a set number of days (as I recall, seventeen) a year. Or as a UUP leaflet had

---

* Revised – after those heavily trailed allegations of Paisley's funding the UVF in 1969, and newly unearthed footage of Martin McGuinness overseeing the loading of explosives into a car in Derry – to Chuckle Bombers.

it, seeing to it that the flag was 'ripped down' for the rest of the time.

The ensuing 'flag protests', which stretched from the end of 2012 well into 2013, were particularly unpleasant – and, you would have to say, singularly stoked – in the east of the city, leading to riots on the edge of Short Strand and petrol bomb attacks on Naomi Long's constituency office on the Newtownards Road. Long herself received a death threat. Large crowds would gather every Saturday on one of east Belfast's most famous shopping streets, Bloomfield Avenue, to march on the City Hall. (Shoppers, not surprisingly or unreasonably, started giving the street a wide berth. A number of small businesses there – women's boutiques in the main – shut permanently. But, you know, a principle's a principle.) Although Naomi Long actually increased her vote in 2015, the DUP – in the shape of Gavin Robinson (no relation to Peter) – retook the seat (it seems reasonable to conclude) with the help of votes from working-class Protestant areas, of the kind Naomi Long herself comes from. His acceptance speech was a masterclass in gracelessness:

> I'm delighted that the last five long years are over. I'm delighted that a new day has dawned in east Belfast... When the people of east Belfast were asked to vote for a shared future, they chose to share it with someone they could trust, rather than back a party that are only interested in sharing a future if we share their view.

A YouTube parody – 'Gavin Robinson Acceptance Speech, AD 1690' – consisted of a clip of Shrek roaring, villagers quailing and DUP-ers chuckling and applauding, as they had applauded and chuckled at the speech itself. Robinson was, I am bound to add, contrite the day after – the day and all that adverse publicity after – and Peter Robinson did contact Naomi Long telling her he was sure she would bounce back.

He wasn't wrong.

What is most dispiriting, contemplating this track record of illiberalism and intolerance, is that in the late eighteenth century, northern Presbyterians – in the town (as it was then) of Belfast in particular – were among the most radical and reform-minded on the island of Ireland.* To them we owe the city's first museum (and the first on the island to be paid for by public subscription) and the Belfast Society for Promoting Knowledge, better known as the Linen Hall Library, which carries on to this day, a link to those enlightened times. Belfast was the first town to send congratulations to revolutionary Paris. (I like the thought of Robespierre and Danton sitting at breakfast, opening mail… 'Oh, look, it's from Belfast. Isn't that sweet.') A group of its most prominent radicals, in the company of Wolfe Tone, a Dublin lawyer, climbed to the peak of Cave Hill, overlooking the town, and made a pledge to unite all Irishmen – Catholic, Protestant and Dissenter.

If that was a high point (and it still doesn't get much higher for me), the Rising they embarked on in 1798 was one of the

---

* Aodán Mac Póilin: Belfast in the late eighteenth and early nineteenth centuries was 'as far ahead of its time as it now is behind'.

lows, descending as it did, in several parts of Ireland, into exactly the kind of sectarian strife they stood against. The Act of Union, which created the entity and the term 'United Kingdom of Great Britain and Ireland', was introduced in the wake of the Rising. Little by little, the North became better known for its industry than its radicalism. The very thing that the eighteenth-century Presbyterians had dreamed of became the nightmare scenario of their descendants.

That's where all the U's come in to our political parties. The appeal to the Protestant vote became a competition as to who loved the Union most, or – pointing the righteous finger at your opponent's failings – who didn't love it half enough.

The DUP's emergence as the leading party of Unionism was based on its convincing enough Protestants, in the years after the Good Friday Agreement and the setting up of the Northern Ireland Assembly, that the UUP loved the Union less than they did. It would be wrong to think that any significant proportion of the people who voted for them were themselves, say, creationists, or were even, many of them, opposed to same-sex marriage or abortion reform, in the same way that it would be wrong to claim that all Labour voters were inherently anti-Semitic because some of Jeremy Corbyn's supporters are. And – all of this has been leading up to – it was on the Union that their Referendum campaign was run.

So enthusiastic was the DUP in promoting its Leave message that it took out a front page ad in the *Metro* newspaper – unavailable in Northern Ireland – at a cost of over £250,000, part of the £425,000 it spent in the course of the Referendum campaign, compared with just under £60,000 spent on the 2015 general election. The money was a donation from the pro-Union Constitutional Research Council, which also helped fund the ultra-Brexit European Research Group.*

Arlene Foster greeted the June 2016 result by saying, in the vein of Ian Paisley after the 1998 Referendum, how proud she was of the people of Northern Ireland... presumably for being one of only three regions (with Scotland and Greater London) where Remain votes outnumbered Leave: 'We are now entering a new era of an even stronger UK.'

And never mind that there were people queuing up to tell her and her party the opposite: Brexit was bound to complicate matters; Brexit was likely to cause some of the people who had been content to accept the Northern Ireland envisaged in the Good Friday Agreement and who had voted Remain in the Referendum to wonder whether their interests and aspirations wouldn't be better served in a United Ireland. Martin McGuinness, in fact, called for a 'Border Poll' the day after the Referendum (a vote, in other words, on Northern Ireland's continued inclusion in the United Kingdom, or, as it is more often talked of here, on a United Ireland).

Peter Robinson – unencumbered by leadership these days – speculated on the morning after the poll whether reunification

---

* Dating back to the Troubles, when there would have been concern for the safety of donors, details of donations to political parties in Northern Ireland were not made public in the way that they were in the rest of the UK. Legislation to bring us into line was introduced at the end of 2017. Initially, it was thought that this would be backdated to include all donations from 2014, that is before the EU Referendum. The DUP lobbied – successfully – for a later start date of 1 July 2017.

was an outcome, or at least a debate, that the party ought to be beginning to prepare for. Even more surprisingly, perhaps, Eileen – now Baroness – Paisley, recently averred that a reunited Ireland might not actually be a bad idea, carrying on the journey begun by her late husband out of Neverneverneverland. Indeed, she went further and wondered whether 'going right back to the beginning' – that is to say, to 1920 and the Government of Ireland Act – it might not have been a mistake create a border in the first place. 'I just wonder,' she said, 'why [the island] had to be divided at that time and I think that was the wrong division. It is too big an issue for me to pontificate on.'

(On other subjects, mind you, the Baroness's views were rather more traditional. Asked about Alison Bennington, who just a few weeks earlier had taken a seat in the Antrim and Newtownabbey Borough Council elections, becoming the DUP's first openly gay elected representative, she replied, 'That girl may not know Christ died for her.' The decision to select her was, she suggested, 'a decision taken at the time and I think it was taken as a defiance to see what would happen. And I think it should be put to the whole party and a proper decision made on what should be done.'[2])

Her son, Ian Paisley Jr, was warm in his appreciation of Martin McGuinness on the retirement of the former Deputy First Minister, thanking him 'honestly and humbly' for his work. Although defending his father's legacy, which indirectly his praise did, might have been expected of a person dubbed 'Baby Doc' by members of his own party (Paisley Jr stepped into the parliamentary seat Paisley Sr had vacated in 2010), he did indeed sound both honest and humble. I don't think I was alone in sitting up and thinking, just... wow. This too though is in a different register to his comments on, for instance, LGBT matters, as in this 2007 interview with Dublin-based magazine *Hot Press*: 'I am pretty repulsed by gay (sic) and lesbianism. I think it is wrong. I think that those people harm themselves and – without care about it – harm society... I mean, I hate what they do.'[3]

Alone of the five main Northern Irish parties, the DUP has no clear statement of its position on Brexit on its website, which is, to say the least, curious given that their wishes on the subject have coloured so much of the debate in the past two or three years.

They do, though, have a Brexit spokesperson in the shape of Sammy Wilson, or as Belfast businessman Bill Wolsey (owner of the Merchant Hotel, and ardent Remainer) calls him, 'Tsunami' Wilson. Sammy loves to shout from the terraces, a skill he honed as a Belfast City Councillor in the 1980s, when the council chamber was regularly referred to as a 'bear pit'. ('Poofs' and 'perverts' he called a gay rights group applying to use the City Hall in the early 1990s. Irish, meanwhile, was a 'leprechaun' language.)

He's sixty-six now but still looks and sounds like the wee lad with the bigger mates who slabbered at you from the back of the bus. (The current Irish Taoiseach is, variously, 'Vile Varadkar' and 'Vacuous Varadkar'.*) It was Sammy Wilson

---

* I was a bit of a slabber myself – and as it happens went to the same school. I recognize the traits. If only I'd had mates.

who, on hearing concerns raised in the House of Commons by Ian Blackford of the Scottish Nationalist Party about rising prices and food shortages in the event of a no-deal Brexit, shouted that people could always go to the chippy. It took a Belfast chippy owner to point out to him that, as far as Sammy's own constituency was concerned, nothing actually grew in Northern Ireland in the winter, so everything, including the potatoes for the chips, had to be shipped in:

> Our chicken comes from Holland, our fish comes from big trawlers out in Iceland and Norway. Most of the potatoes come from Southern Ireland, which is in the EU, and our onions for onion rings are Spanish onions because they are so big... If the potatoes and the veg and the fish aren't in the shops, they aren't going to be in the chippy either... I don't know where he thinks we are going to get it from. Does he think we are going to grow it in our own back yards?[4]

(The answer is that he quite possibly does, since he's so fond of invoking the Second World War: 'If the Luftwaffe and the Wehrmacht couldn't starve us, I don't think a bunch of Brussels bureaucrats with their customs forms are going to.')

Previously, Sammy had appeared to agree in a filmed insert for a current affairs TV programme with a member of the public who said that Brexit was necessary to 'get the ethnics out'. Sammy denied the accusation: it was only the first bit – the necessity of Brexit – he was agreeing with, which is about as plausible as the time I told my brother when I had drunk the whole of a glass of juice we were to share that my half was the bottom half and I had had to drink his to get at it.*

This is a man who as Environment Minister in the Stormont Executive, in 2008, banned the broadcast of Westminster-sponsored ads urging UK citizens to cut their carbon emissions, on the basis that global warning was all – a favourite Sammy Wilson term, this – a con. Or to quote his own website: 'Climate change is not man-made and the myth of climate change is based on dodgy science not proven.' Mind you, it says something too about the way our Executive works that a minister could make a decision – a pronouncement – like that without check or the need for a collective discussion. And while we're on science, Sammy is categorically not a member of the DUP's creationist tendency: see his speech to the December 2018 Leave Means Leave rally, at which he has a go at the European Court of Justice for its ruling that the UK could extend Article 50 independently of the other twenty-seven states. 'Here's an organization that normally works at about the same pace as evolution and it made a decision within four or five days.'

In 2010 – in his capacity as MP for East Antrim – he organized an event in a Westminster committee room called (catch the jeer in the title) 'Climate Fools' Day, in memory of the passing of the Climate bill on 29.10.08.†

It's not a fight Sammy likes, so much as a goad. And a man

---

* Like I say, a slabber.
† Sammy's website says he is well known for his sense of humour. That'll be what that is, then.

in Number 10. Big mates don't come much bigger than Boris Johnson (PM and MU). Since the end of July, Sammy has been telling anyone in the EU – and in the Irish government especially – who will listen that they're going to get what's coming to them now, all right. 'It's a different regime,' he trumpets. You show them your big mate can show them, Sammy.

It would be wrong to suggest that Sammy was a complete fool. A *Belfast Telegraph* article on the eve of his departure from the Finance Ministry (where he had moved from the Environment), due to a bar on people holding seats in Stormont and Westminster both – so-called 'double-jobbing' (triple in Sammy's case: he still put in a shift at the erstwhile bear pit of Belfast City Council) – included several endorsements of his abilities and, indeed, his tell-it-like-it-is manner. 'Sammy Wilson goes from Figure of Fun to Principal Player' was the headline.[5]

It is perhaps too easy to mock (not to say overstate) the DUP's fusion of faith and fundamentalist politics. In fact, as a leaked 2008 memo from the US Consulate in Belfast to the State Department acknowledges, the DUP contains 'many diverse elements'. And yet there is genuine substance to the stereotype. William Irwin – elected MLA for Newry and Armagh in 2007 – told a newspaper at the time of that campaign that he entered political life after his fifteen-year-old son drowned in a swimming pool accident. Ian Paisley visited the family and prayed with them. 'It gave me a new perspective on life,' Irwin said. 'I wanted to put something back into the community.'[6]

In an odd twist, William Irwin was replacing Paul Berry, himself a prominent gospel singer, who had been suspended from the party following a newspaper story that he had met a man in a Belfast hotel for what was coyly described as an 'intimate massage'. Speaking a few years later when the DUP leadership was dealing with a far more damaging story, Berry remembered being summoned to Paisley's house for a meeting with the party leadership, 'I was forced on to the street by Peter Robinson... The DUP seniority has always been ruthless. Other parties try and help their members if they are in trouble – but not the DUP.'

That more damaging story, of course, was the one involving Peter Robinson himself and that affair between Iris Robinson and Kirk McCambley. Robinson stepped down as First Minister – making Arlene Foster the first woman North or South to head (or half-head) up a national assembly – while the claims against him were investigated and eventually dismissed. Iris Robinson was, however, found guilty of a serious breach of the Northern Ireland Assembly's code of conduct. Peter returned to politics. Iris never did. She was expelled from the party in 2010 and underwent a period of what was termed 'intense psychiatric care'.[*7]

And the DUP put scandal behind it. Until Jonathan Bell came

---

* Irish Robinson had previously caused outrage when in the course of a radio interview, she referred to homosexuality as an 'abomination'. That interview is the starting point for a new piece of musical theatre by Conor Mitchell, taking time out from his campaign of works – *opera*, indeed – in response to Brexit. The piece, called (what else?) *Abomination*, takes its audience through ten years of the DUP's pronouncements on equality, verbatim.

centre stage, kneeling in a TV studio while two preachers (in rain-coats!) laid hands on him in prayer, before giving an interview in which he detailed how public money had been squandered – and quite possibly embezzled – with the knowledge of his own party, and very particularly his own party leader, through the RHI scheme.

What a Carve-up

Stormont (2)

Northern Ireland is governed, internally, by a *consociational* Legislative Assembly – that is to say, power is shared by representatives of different or antagonistic social groups (*OED Shorter*), whether they like it or not.

The two parties who have dominated for longest the Executive and the positions of First and Deputy First Minister seemed, for the best part of a decade, to like it quite a lot. The number of ministries allocated to each party is determined by the D'Hondt method, which operates in more than thirty other territories worldwide, including Scotland and Wales, though elsewhere it is the number of representatives in the Assembly, rather than the number of seats at the cabinet table, that are so determined.

Our D'Hondt system requires that all MLAs designate themselves as Catholic, Protestant or Other, which is a bone of contention for some. The largest parties get first dibs, which for the past thirteen years has largely meant the DUP and

Sinn Féin making a grab for Finance and Economy. There is an element of noughts-and-crosses – exie-osies, as we prefer – about it: closing off one route sometime leaves you open to another. There was uproar among Unionists in an earlier Assembly when Sinn Féin plumped for Education and installed as minister Martin McGuinness. Virtually his last act before the suspension of the Assembly in 2002, following the uncovering of an alleged IRA spy ring at Stormont, was to abolish the Verbal Reasoning Test, aka 11-Plus, for post-primary education. (A decision a good many of us here had been rooting for, for years.) Unfortunately, he didn't have the time, or the forethought, to put anything else in its place or explain how pupils were supposed to move now from one stage of their education to the next, with the result that grammar schools began to offer entrance exams of their own devising. Or rather, Protestant grammar schools banded together to offer one lot of exams (three papers in total), Catholic grammar schools another lot (two papers), so that now some ten- and eleven-year-olds, whose parents want to cover all the bases, can be faced with five papers in the November and December of their final year of primary school – a system that has been cited as increasing segregation not just on religious but also economic grounds, the single biggest predictor of whether children will go to non-grammar schools being whether they are in receipt of free school meals.

The Justice Ministry has up to now been omitted from the grab, it being one of the articles of the St Andrews Agreement that the post would be elected by cross-community vote, pretty much ruling out either a DUP or Sinn Féin minister, or any too-strong shade of Orange or Green for that matter. The Alliance Party – the epitome of otherdom – was the obvious candidate, and held the post from the devolution of policing and justice powers in 2010 until 2016 when – exasperated by the tightening grip of the DUP and Sinn Féin on most of the instruments of government – they joined with the SDLP and the UUP in deciding to leave the Executive and form an official opposition. There followed a temporary scramble to form a government until Clare Sugden, an Independent Unionist, was identified and voted in by the DUP and Sinn Féin, taking up her post three months short of her thirtieth birthday. It's tempting to say that if she hadn't existed, the DUP and Arlene Foster, and Sinn Féin and Martin McGuinness, would have had to invent her, but in fact she was well able for them both. She accused them of 'posturing' and 'feathering their own nests in terms of keeping their own constituents right' when that Renewable Heating scandal broke, and questioned why Sinn Féin, which had 'long held values that we don't punish someone without investigation, without knowing the facts' (I only read the reports, I can't vouch for the straightness of her face), was calling for just that in the case of the First Minister, who it wanted to resign. 'Arlene and Martin may have reneged on their responsibilities to do their jobs, but I will not be doing that,' she said, 'because I have integrity.'

And of course, the First Minister not being able to exist without the Deputy First Minister, as soon as McGuinness went, so did the Executive.

★

I understand our politics can be exasperating. I really do. (They bug the hell out of me.*)

In the course of a discussion about Brexit (I caught it on YouTube, my algorithm now offering me Brexit discussions in the way it once offered me Teenage Fanclub John Peel Sessions), Professor Brigid Laffan, Director of the Robert Schuman Centre for Advanced Studies at the European University Institute, Florence, says, with something close to disbelief, that 'the DUP didn't want the Good Friday Agreement. They didn't sit in those negotiations, they opposed it, they opposed it in the Referendum and now they're the ones with the political power over that part of Ireland.'

Which is perhaps mixing up two not entirely related things. The DUP are the ones with political power over this part of Ireland in the sense that they are the ones giving the Conservatives their single-finger working majority.† That is because they have ten of our eighteen MPs, which they gained with 36 per cent of the vote in the last general election – a 10 per cent swing from the election before that and a full 6.5 per cent more than the next nearest party, Sinn Féin. (On the day that Boris Johnson prorogued parliament, Sinn Féin reiterated their abstentionist policy saying, seriously, what's the point of taking your seat if you and the other 640-odd can be turfed out that easily?‡)

---

* I say 'the hell' obviously because I hardly fucking know you.
† From this line alone will you be able to plot the precise moment of my writing this page. By the time I stood waving it off to copy-editing that majority was a minority of 40.
‡ In the autumn of 2018, those ten DUP MPs were temporarily nine

But Professor Laffan is right in terms of Northern Ireland's devolved administration: the DUP didn't vote for the Good Friday Agreement. They looked at one stage as though they might be forced by it into full-blown retreat. So, either they did something remarkable or someone obviously fucked up somewhere along the way.

Or the British and Irish governments entered into a subsequent agreement with 'the parties', but in reality with the DUP and Sinn Féin, that everyone else in the world appears (reasonably: you have enough on your plates) to have forgotten, which created the conditions for those two parties to enter into government together.

It is difficult now to remember but the first power-sharing Executive here was led by the UUP and the SDLP. Their party leaders – David Trimble and John Hume – shared the 1998 Nobel Peace Prize. (Though it was Hume's own deputy, Seamus Mallon, who was lower-case 'd' to Trimble's O in the FM combo.) Bono called them on stage – in their shirt-sleeves! – during a 'Yes' gig in Belfast's Waterfront Hall in May 1998, ahead of the Good Friday Agreement confirmatory referendum, and raised their hands above his head. 'Two

---

when Ian Paisley Jr was suspended from parliament – and the party – following the revelation that he had accepted (and failed to declare) an all-expenses-paid family holiday from the Sri Lankan government, on whose behalf he subsequently lobbied parliament. Bizarrely, he claimed in a *Daily Telegraph* interview to have gone there to discuss possible post-Brexit trade deals. In 2013. Clearly he knew something none of the rest of us did. And clearly he was doing something similar the following year when he accepted another holiday to the Maldives paid for in part by a cabinet minister there.

men, taking a leap of faith, out of the past and into the future.'*

Even at that stage, though, much of the energy and interest of the British and Irish governments was devoted to the parties then standing third and (most particularly) fourth in the polls, the party, that is, doing the invisible three-legged race with the organization that had the capacity to explode one-tonne bombs in the centre of London.

In the years that followed, the governments' determination to keep that party in the process, no matter what, exposed the 'coalition of the centre' on both flanks. The UUP were called out repeatedly by the DUP for their stance on continued IRA activity and the foot-dragging over arms decommissioning. The SDLP for their part doubled-back so often to make sure Sinn Féin were keeping up – or not being left behind – that when the latter suddenly burst past them, they had nothing left in the tank with which to respond.

The real carve-up – the moment that our Assembly politics took on the shape they have retained right down to today – was ushered in by the St Andrews Agreement. The Assembly had been suspended for four years, since 2002, dissolved in fact, and Direct Rule from London had been reintroduced. And here it is maybe worth taking a second to reflect that of the twenty years since it first met (it existed in shadow form for a year before full powers were devolved in December 1999), the Assembly has been suspended – or dissolved – for getting on seven and

* Stuart Bailie devotes an entire chapter to this gig in *Trouble Songs*, as well he might: he MC-d it.

a half of those years. The current hiatus still has a couple of years to go before it catches up on the 2002 breakdown, which occurred after the uncovering of an alleged Provisional IRA spy ring within the Parliament Buildings at Stormont. The Sinn Féin (and IRA) member at the centre of the allegations, Denis Donaldson, a close associate of Gerry Adams from their days in Long Kesh (later, Her Majesty's Prison Maze), was subsequently exposed as a British agent – or exposed himself, as it were, at a press conference, flanked by Adams and Martin McGuinness – and took himself off to the wilds of Donegal where he lived alone in a house without electricity or running water and where, just four months later, in April 2006, he was murdered by a member, or members, of the *Real* IRA (the IRA, of whatever designation, being, in the matter of informers, merciless, and not in the least concerned with due process).

At times, the whole history of our Assembly reads like a novel by a writer whose desire for plot twists far outstrips any interest in health or education, the mundane business of government. During those years after 2002, the DUP and Sinn Féin overtook the UUP and the SDLP. When it came to St Andrews, therefore, Sinn Féin and the DUP were now the main negotiators and (though all the other parties did sign up too) the document largely reflected those parties' concerns. (In one telling comment, David Ford, leader of the Alliance Party at the time, said his party would not be able to recommend the Agreement to its supporters 'without more detail of what exactly was agreed' – *he was supposed to be in the fucking talks* – especially in 'side deals' between the governments and the DUP and – separately, that is – Sinn Féin.) As well as the headline-grabbing paragraphs on the devolution of policing and criminal justice – and the commitment of Sinn Féin to endorse the Police Service of Northern Ireland (PSNI) – there were also changes to, among other things, the way the First and Deputy First Minister were appointed and to 'community designation': the obligation on MLAs to declare themselves as Unionist, Nationalist or Other. In the political landscape of the early 2000s, Other was pretty much synonymous with the Alliance Party, though there was also a single Green MLA... The 'other' kind of Green, that is.

As Mick Fealty, founder of the independent news and opinion platform, *Slugger O'Toole*, wrote recently:

'It's important to view these two parties as a twosome, not least because that it is how the two governments have dealt with them from the negotiations at St Andrews onwards, and how, in turn, they've used such exclusive influence to squeeze smaller rivals. The cover offered to the DUP and Sinn Féin by the very confidentiality of those 'side deals', has had two effects. One, smaller parties have struggled for relevance in the eyes of their voters, and two, gradually it swallowed the ground available to them for compromise.'[1]

St Andrews also consolidated the Petition of Concern, a 'safeguard' in the Good Friday Agreement, whereby 'a significant minority of Assembly members' (the figure stipulated was 30 of the 108) could request that a decision be taken on a cross-community basis, that is (according to the text) 'a weighted majority (60 per cent) of members present and voting, including at least 40 per cent of each of the nationalist and unionist designations present and voting' (no room in there for 'others'). The thinking was (the key is possibly in that word 'minority') that it would prevent one 'side' dominating the other, in matters of culture especially.

In fact, it came to be used as a way of vetoing any motion or legislation that was not to a particular party's liking, which is presumably what is to be read into the DUP's message to its supporters that (unlike the old 'lousy' Belfast Agreement) the St Andrews Agreement ensured 'no significant decisions can be taken without unionist approval.'

Its use, if anything, only increased after 2006: 115 times in the most recent Assembly term alone. With more than thirty MLAs of its own during that term (meaning it didn't need the support of other parties), the DUP led the way, raising eighty-six petitions. Sinn Féin (twenty-seven MLAs), with the SDLP, had recourse to the measure on twenty-nine occasions, and all the other parties a not-quite-handful of times each. Notoriously, five of the DUP petitions related to marriage equality, despite the fact that there was a small majority in the Assembly (small, but they would have accepted it if it was Brexit) in favour of reform.

Questioned about this on Channel 5's *The Wright Stuff* in July 2018 – 'How can you use a mechanism that is supposed to help and defend minorities against this [LGBT] minority?' – the DUP's Ian Paisley Jr said that the Petition of Concern was 'given to the parties in Northern Ireland by Tony Blair. So, in his wisdom he handed out this veto to parties to use as they will... and all parties have used that veto on numerous occasions, almost a hundred occasions, for *various pet projects.*' (My emphasis.)

In the absence of true collective decision-making, these 'pet projects' covered all areas of policy divergence between the Big Two in particular, from education to welfare reform, the latter being the subject of no fewer than forty-nine petitions, ending with the proposed Welfare Reform Bill going back to the House of Commons, in November 2015, to be legislated on there. (Shame they didn't think then of doing the same for marriage equality.)*

But here's the (if you'll permit me) *mad* thing. Though Sinn Féin and the DUP have most often used petitions against one another, so to speak, neither has been busting a gut to reform or scrap it altogether. And it's not as though they haven't had their opportunities. To quote the wise and much-missed Aodán Mac Póilin, whose book *Our Tangled Speech* is one of the things currently keeping me sane: 'Northern Ireland's peace process is an attempt to accommodate the irreconcilable.' The odds are stacked against anyone operating under its terms actually doing anything. It does, however, '[provide] ideal conditions for the politics of outrage, swagger and emblematic posturing.' The next crisis is never far away. And the next crisis talks.

There was another round of protracted negotiations at

---

* The Parliamentary Under-Secretary of State for Northern Ireland, Ben Wallace, appeared to refer in the House of Commons in the course of the second reading of the Northern Ireland (Welfare Reform) Bill to an instance of the petition being used in relation to caravan legislation. If it was anywhere else, I would say he might have been joking.

the end of 2014, which produced yet another Agreement, the Stormont House Agreement, which in turn – after a temporary mass withdrawal, early the following autumn, of DUP ministers from the Executive* – and yet more negotiations – begat Fresh Start, in November 2015: 'An agreement to consolidate the peace, secure stability, enable progress, and offer hope.' (There was provision in the Fresh Start Agreement for new guidance on the much-abused Petition of Concern. That process was to be begun by the Executive Office, that is Sinn Féin and the DUP in tandem, putting a proposal to the Assembly Speaker within one month to limit the petition's future use. By the time of the latest suspension, however, that had still not been done.)

As is standard, when parties agree to get back to doing the thing they have been elected to do, namely governing, the US president, his secretary of state, the Irish and British governments praised them for their momentous achievement, though not quite as much as Sinn Féin and the DUP praised themselves. On the anniversary of that agreement, six months after the restoration of the Executive, in November 2016, the DUP and Sinn Féin released a statement advertising the fact that they were getting along famously, complete with photograph of smiling ministers artfully (and pointedly) mingled, and jibes at the parties who had finally given up any hope of being able to influence the Executive from within and gone into opposition

---

* '… mass' but not total: Peter Robinson left Arlene Foster in place as Finance Minister and acting First Minister. After all that acting it was no great surprise when – on Peter Robinson's retirement in January 2016 – she stepped into the role of First Minister full-time… for a year.

('Imagine if we had followed the example of others and decided the challenges of government were just too daunting').

Two months later, Sinn Féin withdrew from the Executive and brought down the Assembly.

The official line is that it was all brought crashing down by the scandal around the RHI scheme. Certainly, it would have been enough on its own to bring any government down.

Renewable heating covered three main forms: solar water heating, 'deep geothermal, ground source or air source heat pumps' (no, me neither) and biomass, or wood pellet, boilers. There were two parts to it: domestic, introduced in 2014, and non-domestic, introduced two years earlier. The latter was administered by Ofgem, the government office for the regulation of the gas and electricity market in the UK.

In Northern Ireland the scheme resulted in hundreds of customers being paid more in incentives for burning sustainable fuel than the fuel itself cost. Very simply (it came to sound like a mantra), 'the more you burned, the more you earned'. The minister responsible for introducing it, at the Department of Enterprise, was Arlene Foster. It has since emerged that at the time she was recommending its adoption to the Assembly, she hadn't read the regulations. As the anomaly came to light and legislation was being prepared to end it, there was a last rush of applications, a number of which came from people related to DUP members and advisers. It was almost as though someone had put the word out.

All this had been known within the Executive Office months

before. Certainly, it had been known when Sinn Féin and the DUP issued that joint statement in autumn 2016, telling everyone (not least the so-called 'smaller parties' – including of course the two largest parties of yore) how brilliantly they were doing in government.

The question of exactly Who knew What When, How they then reacted – and Why – has been the subject of a public inquiry that at the time of writing has yet to publish its findings. The only question that can at present be answered with confidence is *Where* these boilers were located: around a third were in poultry farms, many in Mid Ulster and Tyrone. The largest single recipient had thirteen boilers for his sheds – and his tanning salon sideline – each piped to run off a separate meter to maximize profits, which were expected to total £2.5 million by the time the scheme closed. And he had previously been cited as an example of good practice by the Department of Agriculture (Minister at the time, Michelle O'Neill, now Northern leader of Sinn Féin: her department organized fifty-eight workshops to promote the scheme).[2]

That there was a whiff of more than just burning pellets from the DUP side of the chamber was unarguable. The relatives of one special adviser had eleven boilers between them. Another special adviser – seemingly believing that the money was coming out of the Westminster Exchequer – told a colleague it was an opportunity to 'fill our boots'. (Whatever the findings of the inquiry, its hearings have shone a light on the role of such special advisers – SPADs – at Stormont: co-opted by political parties and having the status of temporary civil servants. Shone a light too on how both the DUP and Sinn Féin regarded the rest of the Assembly. Máirtín Ó Muilleoir, Sinn Féin Finance Minister, told the inquiry that 'it was Sinn Féin's decision not to "yield"' to a bill – passed in the Assembly by a margin of two-to-one, though with the SDLP abstaining – that placed restrictions on who could and could not be a special adviser.*

There was, though, a suggestion that Sinn Féin's decision finally to pull the plug had, as often in the past, as much to do with the party's longer-term ambitions south of the border. And then there was the matter of Martin McGuinness's health. There had been rumours that he wasn't well, of trips abroad cancelled, and he had been out of the public eye for some time, but his appearance on the January afternoon that he called a press conference to announce his resignation as Deputy First Minister was truly shocking. And the sigh he made as he sat down to speak – as though something irrevocable was about to be uttered… It was one of those moments where even those who would not normally give a person the time of day use the phrase, 'I mean on a human level…'

There were other aggravating factors, of which the possible consequences of the EU Referendum was undoubtedly one. The partners in government had campaigned on opposite sides – Sinn Féin countering the DUP's 'Leave makes the Union

---

* Sinn Féin regard the bill – put forward by Jim Allister – as discriminatory in its stipulation that no one with a past conviction could be appointed special adviser. The impetus for the bill was a campaign by Ann Travers, whose sister Mary was murdered by the IRA, against Sinn Féin's appointment of Mary McArdle, who had gone to prison for her role in that murder. Just try that phrase again though: 'decision not to yield' to a bill passed in your own legislative assembly. And you thought you heard it first this summer.

(with Great Britain) stronger' message with a call to 'vote to put Ireland first and vote Remain in the EU'. The Referendum, though, had been and gone several months by the time the two parties' Executive Ministers mingled and smiled for their all-getting-along splendidly snap. Two days before Christmas, with the RHI scandal deepening and relations between the two main parties worsening, the DUP Minister for Communities, Paul Givan, announced – by email to the organization concerned, Líofa – that his department was withdrawing funding for an Irish language scheme that helped some hundred people a year who could not otherwise afford it to spend time in the County Donegal *Gaeltacht* area. ('Happy Christmas,' he signed off, 'and happy New Year.' This a man with a Diploma in Advanced Management Practice.) The impression grew that not only would the DUP never support legislation to recognize the Irish language – another long-running point of contention between them and Sinn Féin (and other parties, it has to be said, in favour of an Irish Language Act) – it would go out of its way to thwart and belittle it. An impression that was reinforced by Arlene Foster's comment (she claimed in relation to Sinn Féin, rather than the demand for an Irish Language Act specifically, as if it made a difference) that if you feed a crocodile it keeps coming back for more.

McGuinness's resignation and his party's refusal to nominate a successor had triggered an election, which saw Sinn Féin come within 1,170 first preference votes* of the DUP – or 0.2

---

* A few of their 224,245 votes were cast by voters dressed in crocodile costumes.

per cent – on an increase of almost 4 per cent, in contrast to the DUP's drop of 1.1 per cent. For the first time in the nearly hundred years since Partition, non-unionists formed a majority in a Northern Ireland Assembly. (That almost seismic shift – journalist Eamonn Mallie in fact referred to it as 'an earthquake' and 'the Fall of the Berlin Wall of Stormont'[3] – drew some of the attention from the fact that the Alliance Party, home of the 'others', gained over 2 per cent of the vote.)

Added to the fact that a majority in Northern Ireland had voted Remain in the EU Referendum, this could look like – and was interpreted as – a rejection of the DUP's stance on Brexit as well. At the June general election called by Theresa May, however, the DUP not only held its ground, it gained more, as again did Sinn Féin. With the exception of a single independent Unionist, in fact, the two parties won all of the eighteen seats on offer. It had taken twenty years but the two parties who provided the First and Deputy First Ministers to the first power-sharing Executive – the Ulster Unionist Party and the Social Democratic and Labour Party – were effectively wiped out as electoral forces.

The BBC map of the results suggests a repartitioned Northern Ireland along DUP/Sinn Féin lines. It also suggests a division – often alluded to in conversation – west and east of the (river) Bann. Actually, if you squint, Northern Ireland looks like a Sinn Féin head wearing a DUP wig. (OK, so you really, really have to squint.)

Of more immediate moment, however, was the fact that the two seats the DUP had picked up gave them exactly the number that Theresa May required to form a minority government. Cue all those cartoons in the London newspapers. Cue all those 'who are those people?' questions. Cue all this that I am writing. (What can I say? Go ask the people who voted them in if you want your money back.)

In February 2018, after the collapse of the (then) latest talks aimed at getting the Assembly up and running again, documents were leaked showing that the DUP had in fact contemplated – indeed, had agreed in principle to – a stand-alone Irish Language Bill. Although it would have stood alone only in the way that members of the Three Degrees or the Supremes stand alone, as two other bills would have been simultaneously introduced (an Ulster-Scots Bill and a Respecting Culture and Diversity Bill). The DUP, perhaps afraid that it would be promoted as a (flashing lights) *Diana Ross and* (smaller print) the Supremes, canvassed opinion at the more vividly Orange end of the political spectrum... and baulked. Then walked.[4]

Sinn Féin might themselves have had some explaining to do, had that deal gone ahead. In their case, why, having foregrounded the broader 'rights agenda' as a precondition for restoring the Executive, they were prepared to go back into coalition with the DUP without any guarantee on marriage equality. (A stance that confirmed the suspicion of some LGBT people I know that the party had all along been using marriage equality as a way of putting the DUP on the back foot.)* And why, despite calls from many quarters for its reform, it seemed happy to return to government with the DUP with that damn Petition of Concern mechanism still intact.

* In Eamonn Mallie's pithy observation, 'Sinn Féin needs to demonstrate that rainbow placards on lampposts were about more than electoral gain.'

The votes in the House of Commons on 8–9 July 2019 in favour of marriage equality and abortion reform radically altered the landscape here, though perhaps with the unlooked-for consequence of putting off even further a resumption of the Stormont Assembly. The Northern Ireland (Executive Formation and Exercise of Functions) Bill seemed at the time it was moved to be a fairly insignificant piece of parliamentary business, a mere formality: Karen Bradley – still Secretary of State for Northern Ireland – seeking a (further) deferral of a date for assembly elections here, an admission that the talks restarted in May were going nowhere and not even fast.

In the growing guerrilla (guerrilla? It's not far off civil) warfare between parliament and the Executive, however, there are no mere formalities any more. Benches that would normally be empty – because nobody, but nobody who doesn't represent the place usually sticks around for Northern Ireland business – were suddenly packed. Opposition MPs tabled amendments to the bill, on – among other things – reform of abortion law and legislation on equal marriage, both of which had hitherto been designated as 'devolved matters'. Both of those were carried (and carried in some haste into law) with the proviso that they would only come into effect if the Northern Assembly was not up and running by 21 October, which some might say was a disincentive to any party in favour of those reforms to go back into government before that date.*[5]

---

* Nigel Dodds, DUP, claimed it was driving a coach and horses through the Good Friday Agreement. There have been a lot of coaches and horses being driven about the place this summer: the only professions a no-deal Brexit will favour: border guards, coach-and-horses drivers, and chip-shop workers.

As Conor McGinn, the Northern Irish-born Labour MP who introduced the equal marriage amendment, said, 'At the minute, however, the Assembly and the Executive exist in the ether, or as a concept, not in reality, so if they cannot make this law, we will make it here, because, as I have said often, rights delayed are rights denied.'

Former BBC journalist and now regular *Slugger O'Toole* contributor, Brian Walker, wrote, 'MPs are for once not prepared to leave out Northern Ireland, or treat it as a weird and semi-mythical place, as if dreamed up by the likes of Tolkien or Pullman and all too suitable as the backdrop to *Game of Thrones*.'*

There were a few more cynical mutterings that opposition MPs might have seen the amendments as a way of having a go at the DUP: some of that Sammy-Wilson-style barracking from the back benches had not gone down well, still less had the self-importance of a party propping up an unpopular government.

The amendments, though, didn't end there. The Northern Ireland Bill soon became something of a supermarket trolley into which opposition MPs – within as well as without the Conservative Party – piled as much as they could fit in the time allowed them. Dominic Grieve, former Attorney General for England and Wales (not forgetting Advocate General for Northern Ireland), succeeded in getting in an amendment calling for the Secretary of State to report back to the House of Commons at fortnightly intervals on progress towards the restoration of the Stormont institutions, with a further requirement that a motion for MPs to vote on be tabled. In the view of the *Independent*,

---

* I'd like it on record that I held off to p. 77 before mentioning it.

'Crucially, this motion will be amendable, allowing MPs to add clauses to rule out no-deal. If the Commons is prorogued at the time, the amendment... states that it must be recalled to sit for at least five days.' *The Times*, meanwhile, quoted Grieve as saying that no-deal would mark the beginning of the end of the Union, making the Northern Ireland Bill a 'perfectly legitimate place to start looking at how one might make sure no-deal Brexits are fully debated before they take place.'

Northern Ireland was now the absolute centre of British politics. Brexit and the attempt to reanimate our long-suspended institutions had overlapped. Which was why early in this book I said that the Northern Ireland Bill might yet turn out to be the most important piece of legislation to come before parliament in a generation... a claim that viewed again from (real-time check) half past ten on 29 August, the evening of the day after Boris Johnson, PM–MU, applied to the Queen to prorogue parliament, sounds, admittedly, as creaky as the Sam's Grill sign in *Bad Day at Black Rock*. The DUP – it almost goes without saying – were the only other party in parliament who welcomed that prorogation.* Arlene Foster declared that it was an opportunity to review her party's confidence and supply arrangement, to ensure that its priorities aligned with those of the government, to which 'Turkeys voting for Christmas' has been one of the milder responses. Turkeys, more like, flogging

* Boris Johnson had not seen fit to tell the Secretary of State for Northern Ireland in advance what he planned to do, even though Northern Ireland, with its own devolved Assembly suspended, would be left in an especially parlous position. It was, in the opinion of Simon Hoare, chair of the Northern Ireland Affairs Committee, an 'absolute scandal'.

all their possessions and moving to this Christmas place with suitcases full of stuffing.

I was in Montreal when the equal marriage and abortion votes went through. You know how it is, you wait and wait and wait for a piece of socially liberal legislation and then the moment you go away, two come along in a quarter of an hour. (Just a couple of days before I left, I was watching a BBC NI current affairs programme in which a leading marriage equality campaigner said he and his partner were going to have a civil partnership, seeing no prospect of legalization any time soon.) My elder daughter was unconvinced. 'I'll believe it when I see it,' she said. Not quite eighteen years she has lived here. Scepticism already runs deep.

In Northern Ireland, after those Commons votes, attention focused again on the Irish language. There is a plain obligation in the St Andrews Agreement for an Irish Language Act, though the DUP has long tried to dismiss it as an annex (three-quarters of the agreement consists of annexes), added without their being consulted.

Since the Stormont House and Fresh Start agreements, that obligation has become – under the heading 'Outstanding Commitments' – an endorsement on the part of the British and Irish governments of 'the need for respect for and recognition of the Irish language in Northern Ireland, consistent with the Council of Europe Charter on Regional or Minority Languages.'

An altogether more slippery form of words, the exact interpretation of which the DUP and Sinn Féin continue to squirt

(I am truly sorry I started on this sentence) back and forth between them. In brief, Sinn Féin will not return to Stormont until the Irish language issue is dealt with, while the DUP say that Stormont is the proper place for the issue to be dealt with: come back in and we can sort it out there.

From Montreal I travelled with my family to Ottawa where, on the night of 12 July – of all nights – I stood in front of the Parliament Buildings (which bear more than a passing resemblance to the Palace of Westminster) watching a show called *Northern Lights*: a moving-image projection onto the façade, which was, essentially, a history of the federation, with accompanying commentary, in English and in French. Words in it, indeed, to the effect that Canada's two languages are its peculiar and particular strength. Canada, it has to be said, has this language thing down pat. 2019, significant anniversary of so much at home, marked fifty years there of the passing of its Official Languages Act. The bilingual street signs, the packaging… it's as much about design as anything. You can look at them whatever way you want. Listening to the commentary up at the Parliament Buildings in Ottawa, I am not entirely sure that the French and the English are direct translations of one another. Each seems at moments to be advancing the story a little, a sleight of hand, or ear, perhaps (my spoken French is not that good and yet I feel somehow I am getting it all), and I think of the times I have listened to the poet Doireann Ní Ghríofa – the way she moves when she reads, and sometimes speaks, between Irish and English, never saying 'and now I am translating from this one to that one' – so that I can nearly believe that I speak Irish. I don't.

★

My younger daughter (who like her sister has a little Irish learned from my wife, who brought it with her from Cork★) is teaching herself sign language while she is on holiday. She tells us she has opted for British sign language (BSL) over Irish (ISL) and asks us if there is a Northern Irish variant. We don't know. We look it up and, unsurprisingly perhaps, the answer is yes, or no, depending on who you ask. It is generally agreed that there exists a distinctive local usage – a marriage of ISL syntax and the BSL lexicon, but some, including the UK government (which recognizes ISL and BSL in Northern Ireland), refuse to accept that this merits the designation NISL.

We wonder which of the two (or three) is used in Stormont, the courts or whether both (or all) are. We read up on the efforts of people in the deaf community to have a sign language act introduced in Northern Ireland: Scotland has one, the Republic of Ireland too, but, as the BBC reports, 'without a functioning Stormont assembly, legislation for sign language in Northern Ireland cannot be introduced.'

The Department of Culture, Arts and Leisure estimates that there are 17,000 severely or profoundly deaf individuals in Northern Ireland. Of this deaf population, there are 5,000 who use sign language as their preferred means of communication: 3,500 use BSL and 1,500 use ISL (Department of Culture, Arts and Leisure, 2011). Another survey suggests that of '7,000 users

★ That would be Munster Irish, the Queen's Irish as my wife jokingly refers to it, a very different thing from Ulster Irish.

of sign language in Northern Ireland, approximately 2,000…
use ISL and 5,000… use the Northern Ireland sign variety that is
referred to by various groups as BSL, BSL-NI, NI-BSL, and NISL.'

There are echoes in all of this of the debates around Ulster-
Scots (does it merit the label 'language' at all?), on which Aodán
Mac Póilin is equally forensically – and occasionally irreverently
– insightful and enlightening. 'Linguistic conflict in Northern
Ireland may be unique in that only a small proportion of the
population can speak Irish or Ulster Scots, and fewer again
speak either on a regular basis.'

The suspicion of the Irish language among unionists is that
it is not just about the Irish language. Sinn Féin has repeatedly
hinted at other agendas. That doesn't mean that there are other
agendas. In fact, the hint is more than enough to wind some
unionists up, which might itself be the agenda. As Aodán Mac
Póilin said, 'in the political culture of Northern Ireland, opposing sides tend to believe each other's propaganda.'

Mac Póilin was as tireless and passionate (and humorous)
an advocate of the Irish (or any) language as you could hope
to meet, and as clear-sighted as anyone I have heard or read:
'[t]he Irish language movement… contains some of the finest
people I have ever met, but it also has its fair share of tunnel-
visionaries, messiahs, linguo-masochists, uber-grammarians
and grant pimps. And I haven't even started on the politicians.'

I first met him while making a documentary ('More of it
Than we Think') for BBC Northern Ireland in the mid-1990s
on the subject of Protestant culture, in the course of which he
cheerfully reminded me – and whoever had not been moved
by that documentary-on-Protestant-culture strapline to switch

to another channel – that northern Protestants played a hugely significant part in reviving the Irish language in the post-Famine years of the late 1800s; that Irish belongs to everyone.*

And it does, whether they live on the island of Ireland or not. There are at the same time many for whom the language is inextricably bound up with their sense of Irishness. It is not a question of them politicizing the language, but of the language occupying a space in their political outlook. *Our Tangled Speech* highlights several examples from a pamphlet issued in the 1980s by Sinn Féin's Cultural Department, conflating the Irish language with the thirty-two-county republican project: 'it is our contention that each individual who masters the learning of the Irish language has made an important personal contribution to the reconquest of Ireland'; 'every phrase you learn is a bullet in the freedom struggle.' That, both the individuals quoted (one is a friend of mine) might with reason say, was then: we are living, and speaking, in changed times. They might though recognize that it may take some people a little more time to shake entirely the feeling that by embracing the language they are betraying their own political beliefs.

But we are the more, all of us, for our several languages.

A Canadian postscript. Most evenings that we are away I have been listening to my daughters watching *The Good Place*, the

---

* Following my interview with him for the BBC NI programme, he sent me a letter with the etymologies of both our surnames, proving that they were, essentially, one and the same.

Netflix series in which a character, played by Kristen Bell, finds herself against her expectations, and the evidence of her earthly life (up to and including the circumstances surrounding her death*), in a version of paradise.

Possibly.

The entire series might have taken its inspiration from 'Duck Amuck', the 1953 Daffy Duck cartoon scripted by Michael Maltese and directed by Chuck Jones, in which Daffy has to react to ever more preposterous changes to the scenery (snow one minute, palm trees the next) and even to his own body shape – by a pencil-wielding hand that keeps intruding on the frame, and that is finally revealed to belong to Bugs Bunny.

Over the two seasons of thirteen 22-minute episodes of *The Good Place* – there are another thirteen to come; I don't imagine they will change much – the characters engage in repeated discussions about what constitutes the Good Place and who deserves to be in it, as opposed to the Bad Place.

The constant back and forth between the Good Place and the Bad Place bleeds into the things I am reading, into the whole Brexit debate: 'Come on, you guys, I know this isn't perfect, but I need more time to build my case. It's either this or back to the Bad Place.'

We leave Canada for Belfast, with Season Three still ahead of us.

---

* Accident involving supermarket trolleys… there but for the grace of [choose your deity] go we all. And, yes, I am trying hard not to think about that Northern Ireland Bill metaphor.

Up the Ra

(And the La and the Da
and the Vf)

On St Patrick's Day evening 2019, Belfast boxer Michael Conlan entered the ring at the Hulu Theatre in New York's Madison Square Gardens for his featherweight bout with Mexico City's Ruben Garcia Hernandez to chants of 'Ooh-ah Up the Ra'.

(The Ra, if your ma or your da or somebody else's never told you, is a nickname for the IRA.)

To be precise, Conlan entered the ring to 'Celtic Symphony' by the Wolfe Tones, whose chorus is possibly the best-known vehicle for the chant, although the Irish Brigade, from County Tyrone, released the 'SAM Song' – also known, simply, as 'Ooh-ah Up the Ra' around the same time – 1987 – as the Wolfe Tones released their 'Symphony'. (The 'SAM' of the title being the Surface-to-Air Missile launchers the IRA acquired from Libya in the second half of 1986.)

The Wolfe Tones formed in Dublin in the early 1960s, taking their name from the United Irish leader who stood with the

Belfast radicals on Cave Hill and swore to unite Catholic, Protestant and Dissenter. (Ooh-ah, how are you... Talk about bathos?) Songwriter Brian Warfield wrote 'Celtic Symphony' to mark the centenary of Glasgow Celtic Football Club, in whose Celtic Park stadium, aka Paradise, the words 'Ooh-ah Up the Ra' appear as 'graffiti on the walls'. I suppose you could make an argument – Brian Warfield certainly does – for the line being purely observational. An observation repeated six times in a row.*

Commenting in the *Guardian* a few days after the Conlan fight, Una Mulally referred to the 'strange momentum the aesthetics of Irish republicanism are gaining as they are repurposed for a new generation.' 'Ooh-ah Up the Ra', she suggested, had come to be viewed, for a generation that had no direct experience of the Troubles, as merely anti-authoritarian: if not entirely detached from its original context, then far enough removed to render it harmless.

More recently, indeed, the chant – and a couple of hundred years of Irish history – has passed through the looking glass of Limerick's 'Dole-Queue Dadaist' duo the Rubberbandits, whose own 'Up Da Ra' runs:

Paddy Irishman went over to London to box the Queen into
the mouth

* Brian Warfield and his fellow band members went head to head (head to head to head to head) with Fintan O'Toole on RTÉ's *Late, Late Show* back in 2002, much of the discussion centring on the 'Celtic Symphony' chorus: '[the Celtic fans] started it before us,' Warfield says again. And Manchester United supporters have hate-filled chants about the Hillsborough disaster.

He had a load of condoms filled with petrol*
And a sword made out of hash
That he sellotaped to the steering wheel of his mother's face
He met the Queen in the car park of Buckingham Palace
And he cleverly locked her into the boot of an Opel Corsa
In that boot
She smeared the walls with shit
And the Queen starved to death
And that's how the Irish Republic was wan!
Ooh, aah! Up The Ra!
Ooh, aah! Up The Ra!
Ooh, aah! Up The Ra!

As Rubberbandit Blindboy Boatclub explained to Belfast music writer Stuart Bailie in an interview for his book *Trouble Songs*: 'When I was growing up in Limerick, the cool thing to do was to support the IRA. But the kids that were doing it, they didn't know what the IRA was… that's what the song is about, the sheer meaningless of the IRA to a Limerick audience.'

For some people, though, chanting 'Up the Ra' had, according to Una Mulally, become caught up in a reclaiming of Irish identity. 'The IRA is part of the Irish story, whether we like it or not,' she wrote, but acknowledged too, in conclusion (and with a dreadful seeming prescience), that for many others it was 'too soon' to be bandying those words about, 'too dark and too unsettling.'

A couple of weeks later, a member (police think teenage)

---

* Clearly not an early commander of the Provisional IRA… Bide your time.

of the latest incarnation of the Ra – the New IRA – stuck a handgun round a corner of Central Drive in Derry's Creggan Estate and fired a number of shots up Fanad Drive in the general direction of a police Land Rover. One of them struck and killed Lyra McKee, a twenty-nine-year-old journalist who had recently relocated to the city and who had gone with friends to observe the riot that had broken out when police moved in to the area to search for weapons.* In some of the phone footage taken at the scene a voice can clearly be heard shouting, as the gunman appears and takes up position, 'Up the Ra!'[1]

Lyra McKee was one of what were referred to – a little resentfully, she herself wrote – by those who had survived the Troubles as the Ceasefire Babies. (She was four when the Provisional IRA ended its campaign the first time.) Some of her most important work had dealt with the transmission of trauma to that younger generation. First broad- or podcast in January 2016, 'Suicide of the Ceasefire Babies' was a personal and investigative response to figures showing that as many people had killed themselves since the end of the Troubles as had died in them; that there had been a doubling of the suicide rate in that period; and that – while middle-aged people who as children had experienced conflict-related trauma in the 1970s were most at risk, under-25s accounted for getting on for 700, or one in five, of the self-inflicted deaths from 1999 to 2014.[2]

* The only other journalist to be murdered here since the Troubles began was Martin O'Hagan, of the *Sunday World*, gunned down in 2001 as he walked home with his wife by loyalists who had taken exception to his repeated exposés of their less than glorious activities.

(Professor Siobhan O'Neill of Ulster University, in an interview with the BBC in the week of the fiftieth anniversary of the start of the Troubles, reinforced this, saying that children who have parents with mental health issues are more likely to have mental health problems themselves. Figures quoted in the same segment suggest almost 40 per cent of people here experienced a traumatic experience, 14 per cent have a mental illness and 8.8 per cent display symptoms of Post-Traumatic Stress Disorder.)[3]

Lyra McKee was not covering the riot in Creggan in the sense that a journalist in the traditional media would have been: dispatched with the purpose and expectation of filing a story with her by-line. It was more a form of witness. In the online world where she was perhaps best known in advance of the first of the books she was contracted to write, that was or is how journalism increasingly works. Indeed, the most comprehensive footage I have seen of the night's events – before, at the moment of, and after her death – comes from another, what might once have been called unaccredited, source. This in no way invalidates her as either a writer or as a journalist. She had, indeed, been offered a position as a 'desk journalist' by one of Northern Ireland's leading newspapers but preferred to carry on working in her freelance capacity.

She had also, in 2014, written a 'Letter to My Fourteen-Year-Old Self', a response to comments by Pastor James McConnell of Whitewell Metropolitan Tabernacle (the church that out-Paisleyed Paisley's for sheer size) that 'Two lesbians living together are not a family. They are sexual perverts playing let's pretend.' They were the sort of comments which, she had said, 'made fourteen-year-old me feel like I was better off dead, rather than deal with the shame of being gay.'

'It won't always be like this,' she wrote, looking back across the years. 'It's going to get better… You will fall in love… You will smile every day, knowing that someone loves you as much as you love them.'

Which was why she had relocated to Derry a short time before the New IRA murdered her. The New Ra expressed its 'full and sincere apologies' as the Old Ra had often had to do – in July 1988, for instance, when it killed two civilians in an explosion outside the Public Baths on the Falls Road. ('Sinn Féin President Gerry Adams said he had been shocked by the deaths. At the same time, he accepted the IRA explanation that the bomb, intended for a passing British Army foot patrol had been triggered accidentally.' (*Irish Times*))

'In the course of attacking the enemy,' the New Ra statement ran, 'Lyra McKee was killed while standing beside enemy forces.' Never mind the grammar of it (though do note the classic paramilitary use of the passive verb), the morality of it is rank. 'We have instructed our volunteers to take the utmost care in future when engaging the enemy, and put in place measures to help ensure this.'

Politicians and commentators of all stripes were quick to condemn and to emphasize how unrepresentative the New IRA was.

That was the occasion of Alistair Campbell making the distinction between those who provide political analysis to the New Ra and those who had provided it to the Old. As a claim to represent the people, the support of three out of ten of

roughly 50 per cent of the electorate still doesn't seem to me
to be setting the bar that high. Not that the Ra have ever been
bothered by a lack of popular support. It is almost an article of
faith with them that, when all others backslide or compromise
on their republican principles, they hold firm.

IRA logic runs as follows: you do not need majority support
for your violence because you take your legitimacy from the
republic declared at Easter 1916... until, that is, you or your
political representatives, or parties who have traditionally provided you with analysis, or danced with you on the head of
a pin, get majority support; after which anyone carrying on
claiming legitimacy from the 1916 Rising 'speaks for no one'.

The Provisional IRA – the Super or Mainline Ra – was itself
the result of a schism (nearly purged before it had begun) in
December 1969. The narrative runs that what, after the split,
was known as the Official IRA, or something akin to Proto Ra,
had become too interested in left-wing politics, leaving it unpre-
pared to defend Catholic areas when intercommunal violence
erupted in Belfast in that last summer of the 1960s (the mayhem
broke out on the eve of the 'Aquarian Exposition' that was the
first Woodstock Festival: 'three days of peace and music').

The Provisionals – PIRA, as British Army commanders took
to referring to them (think *piracy*, then remove the sea) – were,
at least to begin with, wedded to a much more traditional,
physical force approach to ending Partition. Richard English
in his history of the IRA, *Armed Struggle*, highlights how
socially conservative many of them were. One of its founders,
Billy McKee, attended mass daily. Another leader – Seán Mac
Stíofáin, born in Leytonstone as John Stephenson – refused

to bring condoms from north to south* (where they were unavailable) even though his organization only wanted them to make fuses for acid bombs, which is as messed-up a doctrine on the sanctity of human life as you could wish to read, though in common with all the armed groups here, the Provisionals were to become dab hands at playing fast and loose with that particular doctrine. And, eventually, with condoms too, using them, in November 1991, to smuggle explosives into Belfast's Crumlin Road Gaol, which they fashioned into a bomb, killing rival loyalist prisoners.

Una Mulally in her *Guardian* article also mentions in passing a scene from an episode of the latest Alan Partridge series, first screened in March 2019. Irish Alan-Partridge-lookalike Martin Brennan (played, like Alan Partridge, by Steve Coogan) breaks into a chorus of 'Come out, ye Black and Tans', another song from the Wolfe Tones repertoire, written by Dominic Behan about his father, Stephen, before segueing into the anti-Internment anthem, 'The Men Behind the Wire'. As with all Alan Partridge / Steve Coogan, the comedy is working on several levels simultaneously: in a parody of a British TV chat show a parody Irishman sings Irish Republican songs, while his hosts clap along: it's not clear who the target is, unless it's all of us.

In July, another rendition of 'Come out, ye Black and Tans' was making headlines, sung on this occasion by the Tyrone GAA football team on the bus carrying them from a match in Cavan, which happened upon an Orange march in Aughnacloy,

---

* Thank you for waiting.

a mixed village (almost half-and-half men and women, Catholics and Protestants too) right down on the Tyrone / Monaghan border. By all accounts, the march was uncontentious, an accommodation having been reached in advance between marchers and the local Catholic church, with lodges waiting until mass had ended before proceeding through the town.

The incident – for which the Tyrone manager Mickey Harte unreservedly apologized (an apology, he was glad to say, that had been accepted by 'those who needed to hear') – provoked an interesting discussion on an RTÉ GAA programme, which touched on such things as flags and anthems at GAA games. Touched too on the fact that some of the northern GAA teams are named for – and here the panel are overcome with awkwardness – 'republican martyrs', says one, making speech marks in the air. 'People for whom the other side would have no affection,' says another, and 'republican figures, for want of a better term,' says the third. I'm not sure what the term *is* that they are dancing around…

It is not in the interest of balance or to indulge in what is known here as 'whataboutery' that I feel bound to add that a matter of weeks after the Tyrone GAA incident, the Director of Public Prosecutions decided not to bring charges in relation to a video showing (showing, that is, as in the case of the Tyrone team bus, anyone who went online looking for it) Northern Ireland (football) fans singing 'We hate Catholics… Everybody hates Roman Catholics' to – or approximately to – the tune of Tiffany's 'I Think We're Alone Now', without in this instance so much as a visual prompt.

It is the glee with which such songs are sung that most

depresses, the utter lack of embarrassment. But then again, embarrassment has always been in pretty short supply here. A fortnight after their apology for the Falls Baths bomb, the Provisionals were apologizing again, this time for the murder of the Hanna family – mother Maureen, father Robert and seven-year-old son, David – killed by a 1,000 lb roadside bomb 'intended' for a judge, who, like the Hannas, was returning home from holiday in the US through Dublin airport. Whether the Provisionals would have felt it incumbent on them to apologize for the death of the judge's wife and daughter it is impossible to say, though the organization's response to its murder, in 1984, of magistrate's daughter Mary Travers and attempted murder of her mother as they left mass in south Belfast in the company of their father and husband would suggest not.

Less than thirty-six hours after Lyra McKee was murdered, Saoradh (it means Liberation) – the political organization most closely identified with the New IRA – marched through Dublin, with scores of members – or supporters – dressed in uniforms and berets and wearing dark glasses (curious garb indeed you might think for a political movement). An *Irish Daily Mail* journalist was jostled as he attempted to question the marchers. That's a thing that republican marchers have in common with their loyalist counterparts: they don't like it when you 'break the ranks'. That – unlike pushing journalists around, say, or shooting them dead – really is a violation.

A few weeks later, the New IRA attached a booby-trap bomb to the underside of the car of an off-duty police officer, which he only discovered the next day (a Saturday) when he arrived at Shandon Park Golf Club in east Belfast. Like a gun fired round a corner, there is a chance that a bomb left under a car will kill or injure someone other than the intended target.

So much for instructing their volunteers to take the utmost care in future when 'engaging the enemy'. By the middle of August, barely four months after Lyra McKee's murder, a BBC camera crew was filming Saoradh members with collecting tins approaching cars stopped at traffic lights in Creggan. Filming too hands coming out of car windows to drop a couple of coins in. There were placards on the lampposts: 'Informers will be shot. IRA', 'RUC Informers: they will forget about you, we won't. IRA.' (Note they don't call themselves the 'New' IRA. To their minds, they are *it*, *them*: the Óglaigh. Just as the PSNI are still the Royal Ulster Constabulary, for so many years a legitimate target of the Provisional IRA.)

According to a report in the Belfast-based *Sunday Life* newspaper, the leader of the New IRA, who the paper names as Thomas Ashe Mellon, banned the chief suspect in Lyra McKee's murder (by this stage he was over the border in Donegal) 'from watching television or reading online news reports in case the outpouring of grief following the senseless murder left him emotionally broken.'*4

* Another article goes further and says Thomas Ashe Mellon organized the riot on the night of 19 April and sanctioned the fatal shots being fired. A second leading figure is said to be a former Provisional who was arrested in 1992 in connection with a proxy bombing in which Patsy Gillespie was strapped into his own lorry and made to drive it to an army checkpoint at Coshquin, on the outskirts of Derry, where he and six soldiers were blown to bits.

Presumably, he will not have seen friends of Lyra McKee approach the Saoradh headquarters, Junior McDaid House on Derry's Chamberlain Street, and place hands, dipped in blood-red paint, on the green-painted walls and the white billboard that reads 'Victory to the Republican Prisoners'.

The killer himself might not have been there at that moment, but Thomas Ashe Mellon definitely was: you can see him in the news footage, left of frame (no, not your man with the baseball cap, next to him, with the beard... there), doing his best to look bemused.

Thomas Ashe Mellon is himself the son and grandson of IRA members, whose involvement goes back to the 1940s. It is curious – to say the least – that the will of the Irish people has been in the gift of a relatively small number of families, who have passed it down from generation to generation. In Belfast, both the Adams and Hannaway families had strong links to the IRA going back to the days when it was the Irish Republican Brotherhood, a secret, elitist organization within the Irish Volunteers. (IRB to IRA... maybe they thought they got better with time.) When Gerry Adams Sr and Anne Hannaway married in the late 1940s, it might have been anticipated that that involvement would be passed on, though miraculously it seems to have given Gerry Adams Jr a swerve.

As a Derry teenager interviewed for the study on 'Violence in the Lives of Children and Youth in "Post-Conflict" Northern Ireland' told researchers, 'If you're born into an (name of paramilitary organization) family then like there's a good chance the boys in the family are going to be in the (organization) as well.'[5]

And it's not just in the North that this applies. A *Vice* news feature from 2015 ('The Republic's Dissident Youth: Ireland's Young Warriors') features Dublin members of Na Fianna – think Ra, think Wee Ra – attached to Republican Sinn Féin, closely identified with the Continuity IRA, whose members, in March 2009, shot and killed Constable Stephen Carroll, the first member of the PSNI to die a violent death. (Both the Continuity IRA and Republican Sinn Féin have their genesis in that 1986 General Army Council, which voted to end abstentionism from the Dáil.) There look to be about five Fianna in total in the photo accompanying the *Vice* feature. A couple are in their later teens. One – Brandon – is nine. At one point, he stands so long on parade in a cemetery (you get to hang out in lots of cemeteries) that the blood, as he says, runs from his head and he falls over. Asked by filmmaker Jake Hanrahan* why he joined the Fianna, he says to get the Brits out, and then 'I like marching.' Only later does it become clear that he comes from a 'long republican family' (sic), as does an older boy, Seamus, who delivers an Easter Sunday oration. 'I asked Seamus to join, I'll not tell a lie,' his father says. He didn't like it at first, 'toddled on his merry way', but eventually asked his father if he could rejoin.

A little earlier, his father quipped that, with the voice he had, Seamus would do well speaking from behind prison bars. There is an element of bleak bravado in it, of course ('better

---

* Jake Hanrahan appears also to have been at the riot in Derry in which Lyra McKee was murdered. He told the *Birmingham Mail* that 'she was caught in crossfire', which seems fundamentally to misunderstand the meaning of 'cross': there was only one gunman that night, and bullets were travelling in only one direction.

not let his mother hear me say that,' his father also says), but there is a carelessness too about the life and life-chances of any one individual, even your own son. The Cause first, the Cause always, the Cause, the Cause, whatever the cost.

Here's a question. It is regularly stated that Orangeism prevented working-class Protestants from making common cause with their working-class Catholics. Could it be that militant republicanism – for all the rhetoric – has done the same thing in reverse?

Back in Derry, film-maker Sinéad O'Shea returned over a five-year period to Creggan to make the remarkable *A Mother Brings Her Son to be Shot*. The son in question is Philly O'Donnell, whose mother was given an appointment by the Real IRA – to date the deadliest of the dissident groups – to bring Philly to be 'punished', by being shot in the legs (kneecapped, in common parlance), for alleged antisocial behaviour. 'I had no choice,' she says. 'If I hadn't kept the appointment, they would have done something worse.' And this despite the fact that her husband, Philly's father, is himself in prison for Real IRA activity, namely planting a bomb outside the city's Strand Road police station.*

If anything, though, the shooting makes Philly more hostile to the IRA. The threat of 'something worse' looms again. The people threatening him are 'brought up brainwashed,' he says. 'Their das were in it during the Troubles and they're still carrying on as if there's a war on when there's not.'

Hugh Brady, a community worker and former member of

---

* Shortly after his release from prison, he too is kneecapped.

the Provisional IRA, was interviewed in the same film. He said, '[the] community will never expel armed republicans. The history of opposition to Britain is too long. It's almost instinctive in people. I think it might even be a gene in the Northern Irish.' Later he says that the people carrying out shootings are 'not monsters' but 'people who are our neighbours.' When something has to be 'dealt with' it's dealt with 'very, very professionally.' He is talking about inflicting punishment that would be considered utterly barbaric were it ordained by the British – or any other – state. Victims have a different view: 'they're hoods with guns,' Philly says.

It bears repeating that though it has undoubtedly contributed to a ratcheting up of tension here ('Anyone who wants to see England withdraw from Ireland… should capitalize on any opportunity,' Jude McCrory, Saoradh), Brexit did not create the New IRA, nor did the collapse of the governing institutions because of the whole apparatus of petitions of concern and arguments over RHIs or the Irish language. The New IRA – a union of the Real IRA and a Derry group styling itself Republican Action Against Drugs – had already been going along quite happily, maiming and murdering (including at least two people in internal feuds) for four years before the 2016 Referendum.

Their press statements are signed 'T O'Neill' – as distinct from the Provisionals, who signed theirs *P* O'Neill, suggesting that Ra nom de guerres are like car number plates: they go up through the alphabet and then (depressing thought) back to the beginning again.

Unless, of course, they just stop.

Veteran Northern Ireland watcher and documentary-maker,

Peter Taylor, ended his recent personal *Journey Through the Troubles* (first broadcast on 10 August 2019) back in the city where his professional interest began, in the aftermath of Bloody Sunday: Derry. He ended, very particularly, at a Saoradh march. 'The underlying problem of the Irish conflict,' he says, 'has always been Partition, out of which the Northern Ireland state was created. Until that problem is addressed, I think there will always be conflict.'

But what can 'addressed' possibly mean here, over and above what was contained in the Good Friday Agreement? If it is code for 'removed', then that would appear to put the fate of all of us on the island in the hands of those for whom the first recourse to grievance is violence. Would we, say, have to ask their opinion on the interim federal Irish state I have heard mentioned of late? You will know when you have arrived where we want to go when we stop leaving bombs outside courthouses and shooting blindly up city streets.

It is as though it is accepted that violence is our default setting. There is a telling moment in a repeat screening of a current affairs programme from 1969, which I watched recently, in which John Hume, praising the Civil Rights movement for adhering to its non-violent principles, says, with care, 'Irishmen aren't noted for their non-violence.' You can blame (and I do) the political vacuum, you can blame (and I do) the uncertainty created by Brexit, but you can't ignore the fact that we have consistently lauded those who, 'when they saw no other option' (or some such phrase), 'took up arms'.

Even those of us who are vehemently opposed to a no-deal Brexit, to the possibility of border checks, cannot simply accept that it makes violence inevitable. I don't know about anybody of the rest of you, but I prefer not to shore up the 'analysis' of someone like Brian Kenna, chairman of Saoradh, who said in an interview with Sky News – you can hear the shrug even in the newspaper report of it – that violence would continue while there was a border of any kind.[6] The response of democrats has surely got to be that whatever the outcome, we will refute the argument that there is no other alternative. And we should never ever, ever encourage the belief that violence might actually yet be effective in bringing about political change, as in the comment attributed in late August to an official working for Irish Foreign Affairs and Trade that, 'The Brits got a bit friendlier to us after the [Continuity IRA's] attempt to murder PSNI officers' in a bomb attack in County Fermanagh.

In June of 2019, Billy McKee, one of those Provisional IRA founders, died aged ninety-seven. Central to his status was a night of intense violence, forty-nine Junes previously, centred on St Matthew's Church in Belfast, situated at the point where the Catholic Short Strand and Protestant Newtownards Road meet. (Until recently, the church railings were backed by a high fence – another peace line.) Exactly what did happen that night is the subject of ongoing debate (world, meet Competing Narratives, Competing Narratives, meet world), but at the end of it, three men were dead on the Newtownards Road side and one in Short Strand. McKee – who was himself wounded five times – was one of a number of leading Provisionals who split from Sinn Féin in 1986 over the ending of abstention.

Messages of condolence came from Republican Sinn Féin and Saoradh.

There are many legitimate questions to be asked about why young people – young men in particular – continue to be drawn to organizations like the New IRA, questions about employment and opportunity in places like Creggan. Fifty years and more after the founding of the Northern Ireland Civil Rights Association, four wards in the Foyle parliamentary constituency, including Creggan Central, feature in the top ten most deprived areas in Northern Ireland. And this despite high-profile events – and hoped-for incentives for investment – such as Derry's inauguration as the 2013 UK City of Culture (slogan, 'Let it be LegenDerry'), recalling the words of the late (and indeed legendary) musician and broadcaster, Gerry Anderson, that Derry was a state within a state, 'Monaco without the money.' (A fifteen-year-old in *A Mother Brings Her Son to be Shot* wishes that the Troubles were back again for the purpose they gave, but also because, as he sees it, it was all about having a go at the peelers and the Brits.)

But there are also questions to be asked about the Cult of Ra. Billy McKee lived to be an old, old man but to judge from his public pronouncements, he never wavered in his belief in the cause of physical-force republicanism. He was accompanied on his final journey by men and women dressed in black berets and jackets bearing the legend 'D-Coy' (of the IRA's 2nd Belfast Battalion, that is). D-Company's war included taking Jean McConville, a widow, from her ten children, three weeks before Christmas 1972, transporting her across the border and shooting her, before leaving her body in an unmarked grave for more than thirty years.

At McKee's funeral, a statement was read at a memorial

garden not far from St Peter's Pro-Cathedral where the funeral service had been held. (Television footage shows a city sight-seeing bus in among the traffic held up by the cortège, its top-deck passengers standing, not able to believe their luck: an actual paramilitary-style funeral, complete with black beret and gloves on the flag-draped coffin.) 'For him,' the statement read, '[republicanism] was not for a new Ireland or an agreed Ireland, it was for a 32-county independent republic that was declared in front of the General Post Office in 1916... He stayed faithful, loyal to the Proclamation... unlike those who moved against him.'

If you want a short history of the Ra, that's it.

I know which McKee I would rather have speak for me.

There was disgruntlement in evidence at Billy McKee's funeral, a point being made about Sinn Féin's backsliding, as there was later in the summer at the funeral of another high-profile member of the Provisionals, Alex Murphy (D-Coy again in attendance), who was convicted for the murder, in spring 1988, of two British Army corporals who drove into the funeral of an IRA man killed a few days before at the funeral of three other IRA members murdered a few days before that again in Gibraltar. (A masked man fired shots over his coffin before it left Alex Murphy's home. The cortège paused at the bottom of Northumberland Street, next to a D-Coy mural, declaring, 'Our Struggle Continues', above the one that says the thing about 1919 being the mandate.)

The rhetoric, though, is no different at these funerals and the funeral, in Monaghan, two weeks after Billy McKee's, of Kevin McKenna, former Chief of Staff of the Provisionals.

Gerry Adams gave the oration: 'The future is being written now, and, as we help to write that future, we will not let the past be written in a way which demonizes patriots like Kevin McKenna any more than we would the generations before them.' (Sean O'Callaghan, former IRA man and later informer, claimed he once heard Kevin McKenna say of a murdered policewoman, 'I hope she was pregnant... two Prods for one.') 'I think the men and women of 1916 were right. I think the H-Block hunger strikers were right. I think Kevin McKenna was right. I think the IRA was right, not in everything that it did, but it was right to fight when faced with the armed aggression of British rule.'

Compare this with the Saoradh statement following Lyra McKee's murder: 'We have continually gave [sic] our analysis that ["Crown Forces"] oppression would inevitably be met with resistance, as has historically been the case.'

The Fianna Fáil member of the Irish *Seanad* (Senate), Mark Daly – who earlier this year co-authored a UNESCO report, *Northern Ireland Returning to Violence as a Result of a Hard Border due to Brexit*, based on the findings of his earlier, and equally snappy (fifteen words apiece: count them), *Brexit and the Future of Ireland: Uniting Ireland and Its People in Peace and Prosperity*, on behalf of the Joint Committee on the Implementation of the Good Friday Agreement – talks about the dangers of a 'romanticized view' of the past. In a podcast interview for Forward Together following his report, he warned: 'Young people who have no memory of the Troubles will be exploited by adults who want to achieve their own ends and give this glorified view of the past.'

Try this – Sinn Féin MEP Martina Anderson, at a Hunger Strike Commemoration parade in Strabane in the same Council area as Derry, the first weekend of August: 'As the protesting women, as the hunger strikers proclaimed, in the face of all that pointless British brutality, above which we rose with such dignity, tiocfaidh ár lá, tiocfaidh ár lá, *tiocfaidh ár lá!*' *Our day will come*, three times. Or maybe just really, really, really come.

She had earlier performed a little dance with another woman, wearing a tricolour scarf and looking like nothing so much as the women bedecked in Union Jacks who are a staple of the Twelfth of July. The speech offended unionists, the dance offended relatives of the hunger strikers themselves, as well as other republicans: 'stratospherically beyond inappropriate', one called it.

Me? I'm thinking, would you ever fucking listen to yourselves? *You are writing the scripts for future generations. All they have to do is slot in their own names.*

The day after Martina Anderson's Tiocfaidh ár lá Hunger Strike speech, I bumped into the Revd Ken Newell, a former Moderator of the Presbyterian Church in Ireland, who, in the early 1990s, was involved in secret talks with both loyalist and republican paramilitaries exploring the conditions for a cessation of violence. Ken Newell is a man to whom a sermon comes as easily as a sentence, and as lightly.

He had a great simile this particular day about people and their beliefs being like a tennis ball – you didn't know until they met the racket which way they would bounce. At least, I think that was how it went – he was already on to the next thing. He had been at a talk by the biographer of his old friend, and Redemptorist priest, Fr Gerry Reynolds, at which he was reminded of something Fr Reynolds had said – he shows me where he has written it down – about the Orange Order fighting old battles. (Ken Newell is also a former Orange Order chaplain but more recently was taken to task by Unionist politicians who objected to his assertion that the Order still harboured sectarian attitudes.) His focus suddenly swivels. 'People are talking about Irish unity, but part of Ireland isn't being befriended.' He smiles. 'But something new is coming: new bonds, instead of old battles.'

I add Ken Newell to the things about Protestantism I am happy to own. To Ken Newell too I owe the term – new to my ears – Tohu-wabohu, the Hebrew term for the condition of the universe before the Biblical Creation (a minute to 4004 BC in the Free Presbyterian calendar*), translated into early seventeenth-century English as 'without form and void', or in the Greek, 'chaos'. It becomes my phrase for this entire mad hurtle towards the end of October.

Martin McGuinness was, and did, a good many things in the course of his life. His headstone lists some of them: MP, MLA, Minister. But before all of those, before his name, even, is the word Óglach, volunteer.

Not my loved one, not my headstone, not my life, but I wish it were other.

Just about my favourite film in the world when I was a kid was James Cagney's *Angels With Dirty Faces*. You know the one,

---

* Cheap, I know. I'm not proud. It would surprise me if there wasn't cheaper to come.

starts with Cagney's character Rocky Sullivan and his boyhood pal Jerry Connolly (played by Pat O'Brien) being chased by cops: Rocky gets caught, Jerry gets away; Jerry becomes a priest, Rocky a gangster, who one day walks back into the slum where they both grew up and Jerry still ministers, trying to keep kids of the age they were when their paths diverged out of trouble. After '90 Drama-Packed Minutes of the Most Exciting Entertainment Ever Filmed', Rocky is on Death Row, promising to spit in the eye of the guard who leads him on his last walk to the electric chair. Fr Jerry comes to him, asks him not to go out like a hero but to think of the boys who idolize him.

Rocky refuses and then, at the last minute (the look on Cagney's face as he makes his decision has never left me), relents, screaming and crying, clutching, as it looks, for dear life to the radiator in the execution room. The guard mocks him for his hysterics, 'And the yellow rat was going to spit in my eye.' The boys back in Fr Jerry's club are stunned reading the newspaper report: 'In contrast to his former heroics, Rocky Sullivan died a coward.' It's one of the problems in this part of the world that nobody wants there to be any doubt that they were in fact a hero.

I shouldn't forget in all this Ra talk, the La, as in Irish National Liberation Army – another, later offshoot of the Official IRA, who despite their own belated ceasefire in August 1998 are still around, and killing too. In December last year, they murdered Jim Donegan as he waited to collect his son from school. An indication of their other current activities is to be found in the haul from police raids either side of the border in the early summer of 2019. A PSNI press release lists three weapons – two assault rifles and a sub-machine gun – as well as 'a quantity of Class B drugs, counterfeit clothing and DVDs, approximately £13,000 in cash, phones, tablets, documentation, over 7,000 illicit cigarettes and a quantity of hand-rolling tobacco.' The *Garda Síochána*, meanwhile, in their raid in County Donegal, netted 'about 60,000 illicit cigarettes, a large quantity of tobacco, a large quantity of counterfeit clothing, DVDs and other items including money.'

And then, of course, there are the Loyalists.

One sure way to take the temperature of loyalism is to glance up a lamppost, in a Protestant district of any Northern Irish town, or even townland, starting around the beginning of May.* If you want to know what loyalists are thinking, look at the flags they are flying in the run-up to the Twelfth of July.

This year's Twelfth flags are mainly Union Jacks and huge – the size of bedsheets, some of them – which seems likely to be tied in with Brexit and the conversations it has kickstarted about a (near-)future Border Poll. At times in the past when there has been major dissension between Unionists and the British government of the day, the 'Ulster' Flag has predominated: a red cross, a la St George, 'defaced' (is the heraldic term... *guys, I'm using the heraldic term*) by a six-pointed white star, with a red hand at its centre and a crown perched on the uppermost point of the star.

---

* Although the decision as to what constitutes a Protestant part of town tends to lie with those in possession of the ladders and the cherry-pickers.

The old, perpetually Unionist, Stormont government adopted this as the *de facto* Northern Irish flag in the 1950s but the official 'national' flag was and remains the Union Jack. Our contribution to that is the St Patrick's saltire (red on white background), or presumably 6/32 of it, its incorporation occurring post-Act of Union and pre-Partition.

There are flags celebrating the UVF, which those who put them up are adamant refer to that anti-Home Rule militia that, when the First World War broke out, morphed into the 36th (Ulster) Division of the British Army that suffered such huge casualties at the Somme, and *not* to the revived, clandestine group that in 1966 – three years before the Troubles are generally assumed to have started – began murdering Catholics, or Protestants who they mistook for Catholics, or who stood too close to Catholics at the bar, or who otherwise crossed or peeved them.

On its publication in 1999, the book *Lost Lives* documented 3,637 Troubles-related deaths. The first (John Patrick Scullion), second (Peter Ward) and third (Matilda Gould) murder victims died at the hands of the UVF, in May and June of 1966. The 3,633rd (Frankie Curry), in March 1999, was murdered on the street where Peter Ward died. Curry's uncle had been jailed for that murder and it was, apparently, to Curry's own childhood home that the gang had gone after the shooting. In the thirty-three years between then and his death, Curry had at one time or another been a member of practically every loyalist paramilitary grouping and on his own admission had killed upwards of sixteen people, mostly Catholics, but other loyalists too, in internal feuds, as the result of one of which, finally, he himself died.

★

On one east Belfast thoroughfare in the summer of 2019, a 'Spurs Yid Army' flag complete with Star of David has been flying. There is a possibility that this is a hangover from the Champions' League Final, which Tottenham Hotspur competed in (if it isn't a stretch to say), and lost, to Liverpool, although given the rarity of football flags in these displays, even of those with a traditionally Protestant fanbase like Linfield or Glasgow Rangers, it's just as possible that it's another manifestation of loyalism's pronounced pro-Israeli sentiment. (Loyalism's view of Israel is as a similarly beleaguered state standing firm against attacks from without and within. In republican areas, where the Palestinian flag is popular, Israel is the arch oppressor.*)

Scottish flags are ever popular, Confederate flags not this year in evidence, though not unknown in previous years, but then they are not unknown at Cork GAA celebrations, whether because Cork is the 'rebel' county, or because the flag just has quite a lot of red and white – the Cork colours – or because it was on the cover of Primal Scream's 1994 *Give Out But Don't Give Up* album (which I own and never take down but I wonder about it) or because they are actual supporters of the Confederacy and all it stood for... your guess.

★

---

* There are other pairings: as a Spanish-speaking tour guide tells presenter Mark Carruthers in last year's BBC Radio Ulster documentary *Telling Troubles Tales*, 'you can always find Basques and Catalans in west Belfast.'

110

Not so long ago, UDA flags were almost as numerous as UVF flags, although the two would rarely – if ever – be seen together. The two organizations may both have been represented in the Combined Loyalist Military Command, which declared the Loyalist ceasefire back in October 1994, but they were often engaged in feuds when they weren't (the UDA in particular) feuding internally.

Whatever its continued influence on the ground, on the lampposts of Belfast at least this year the UDA appears to be less of a significant presence. Still in east Belfast, just beyond where My Lady's Road joins the Ravenhill Road, at the corner of Carrington Street, is a UVF mural, a figure in black uniform, black mask, white gloves, holding some sort of assault rifle, while on a hillside behind him a comrade holds a UVF standard. Unusually, it does not take up the entire gable – more a half-page ad, this, with a commercial billboard above that changes every six or eight weeks. Sometimes I think whoever is in charge of the billboard is changing the ads for a laugh. For almost two months this spring – at a time when there was an ongoing case regarding police collusion in the UVF murders of six men at the Heights Bar in Loughinisland, County Down, in the summer of 1994 (or rather, regarding the police's pursuit of the producers of Alex Gibney's latest, and deeply disturbing, documentary *No Stone Unturned*, about collusion in the murders) – the faces looking out from above the hooded men belonged to the stars of *Line of Duty*, handcuffed together, fists clenched, 'Crime Needs an Insider'.

Shortly after that came down, another went up promoting Armed Forces Day 2019 – 'family oriented military events and activities for all ages' including the Military Wives Choir and the Red Hot Chili Pipers. In between times, it was a Tesco's Food Love story: Birdie's 'Everybody Welcome' Jerk Chicken. Last time I looked it was Action Cancer, veteran Northern Irish broadcaster Gloria Hunniford inviting all of us to Paint the Town Pink. I am never entirely sure which way the joke is flowing – up-down, or down-up. Actually, I am not even sure it is a joke. It's like a game of epochal *Misfits* where the bottom half never changes: still here, still here, still here. And not just the mural, the organization it represents.

This year too there are maroon Parachute Regiment flags in among the others. In one traditionally loyalist area close to the city centre, the significance is spelled out: 'Sandy Row stands with Soldier F', that being the code- or court-name of the only British soldier to be arraigned for trial over the murder of thirteen unarmed civilians (a fourteenth died later) in Derry on 30 January 1972: Bloody Sunday. Some of the Parachute Regiment flags have been adapted, with the addition of a Union Jack in the top left corner, an Ulster flag top right and the words 'Londonderry 1972 No Surrender'.

The message calls to mind the gloating graffiti that appeared in loyalist areas – including the housing estate where I grew up – immediately after Bloody Sunday itself: 'Paras 13 Bogside 0'. Seven years later, in the aftermath of an IRA ambush on the Parachute Regiment at Narrow Water, County Down, on the afternoon of the day that Lord Mountbatten was murdered off the west coast of the island, retaliatory graffiti appeared: '13 gone but not forgotten, we got 18 plus Mountbatten'. The number eighteen, along with the Parachute Regiment flag, appeared later in the summer this year on a bonfire in Newry, County Down, on the anniversary of internment, along with the names of a PSNI officer and a prison officer recently murdered by dissident republicans. The Parachute Regiment emblem and the letter F will recur – evermore contentiously – right through the summer, as indeed will references to the eighteen dead soldiers.

In one of the most bizarre incidents of the whole summer – and there are many to choose from – residents in the County Tyrone village of Moygashel complained that their local district council – Mid Ulster – was making the village a 'cold house for Protestants' by deliberately allowing flowers to die in a basket hanging from a lamppost on which were displayed a UVF banner and a banner showing the face of Wesley Somerville, wreathed in poppies, above the UVF badge and the words 'Lest we forget'.

'Questions must be asked of Mid Ulster District Council about why this has been allowed to happen and a full explanation given,' one resident was quoted as saying. Questions about the flowers, not about the banner itself, although the family of a man Wesley Somerville was strongly suspected of killing in nearby Aughamullan in 1974 had earlier criticized the police for failing to remove that banner.*

---

* The Stormont House Agreement made provision for a Commission on Flags, Identity, Culture and Traditions, to report within eighteen months of its being established... and then the Assembly unravelled before the Commission was able to. (Good people on the Commission, but fourteen men and one woman...? What were the Commissioners of the Commission thinking?)

Whatever the truth about that particular murder, Wesley Somerville was undoubtedly involved in the murders of three members of the Miami Showband in 1975. He and another UVF member, Harris Boyle, were placing a bomb in the back of the band's van when it exploded, killing them both and prompting the other members of their gang to shoot the musicians, lined up at the side of the road.

The vast majority of victims of loyalist violence were Catholic civilians targeted – if that is the appropriate word for murders that were often entirely random – for their religion alone. The IRA and other republican groups engaged in sectarian attacks too (the weeks after the Miami Showband massacre saw several particularly egregious examples) and many of the 500 locally recruited police and part-time soldiers killed in the course of the Troubles were Protestant – but the fact remains that loyalists went after unarmed Catholics as a matter of course and with a viciousness that at moments looked gleeful. One notorious killer was said to have sung 'Follow the Yellow Brick Road' as he returned from a murder in west Belfast via his 'favourite' getaway route.

In a scene from *No Stone Unturned*, Patrick Mayhew, then Secretary of State for Northern Ireland, is interviewed at the scene of the murders in Loughinisland and asks what the gunmen who opened fire in the bar that night would say in answer to the question, 'What did you do in your war, Daddy?': 'I shot a man of eighty-seven. He was sitting with his back to me. He was watching the World Cup.'*

---

* It has to be said, this clip is repeated later in the documentary, or at least

The UVF has not in the modern era gone in for the sort of mass shows of strength associated with the rival UDA in the early 1970s, the high-water mark of bush-hat and camouflage jacket sales here. The UDA began as an umbrella organiza- tion for local vigilante groups and at one time claimed 40,000 members. Seamus Heaney paints a vivid picture of those vigi- lante groups in a piece he wrote for *The Listener*, in – and called – December 1971, a time when he found himself, as he writes elsewhere, living on the 'wrong side' (for him, a Catholic) of the Lisburn Road, close to Queen's University.

'They are very efficiently organized with barricades of new wood and watchmen's huts and tea rotas, protecting the territories. If I go round the corner at ten o'clock to the cigarette machine or the chip shop, there are gentlemen with flashlights, of mature years and determined mien, who will want to know my business.'

Staggeringly, and despite it being universally understood to contain within its ranks – if not to be one and the same thing as – the UFF (who justified their Ulster *Freedom Fighters* name by killing upwards of 400 Catholics) and despite too having been included in the 1988 broadcasting ban that saw the words of its representatives, as well as Sinn Féin's, spoken by actors, the UDA was only declared illegal in August 1992, twenty-one

---

that portion of it is where Mayhew says, 'the RUC never give up…' The RUC took a fortnight to bring in for questioning the prime suspects, even though they had had their names since the morning after the attack. Twenty-five years on no one has ever been charged.

years after its formation and two before it declared a ceasefire.

The UVF, though only numbering a few hundred members, has always given the impression that it thinks of itself as the senior organization, which is not to be confused with sober or restrained. It has been responsible for some of the most appalling acts during, and after, the Troubles – *before* it might almost be said: those 1966 murders of John Scullion, Matilda Gould and Peter Ward.

As with dissident republicans, loyalist paramilitaries do not need the excuse of the unsettling effects of Brexit – and the related debate about (in some quarters, clamour for) a Border Poll – to turn their violence on, or up, even though some senior figures did warn the Irish government at the end of 2018 not to indulge in 'Brit-bashing'. (Former UUP leader David – now Lord – Trimble had a few months earlier ticked Dublin off for saying 'silly things' about the border.)

On the last Sunday night in January 2019, five men associated with the UVF in east Belfast attacked Ian Ogle in Cluan Place – the cul-de-sac where he lived and a small spur of the Protestant Albertbridge Road, abutting the Catholic Short Strand – fracturing his skull and stabbing him eleven times in the back. He died at the scene. The alleged leader of the UVF in east Belfast – responsible according to the victim's family for the intimidation and harassment of Ian Ogle in the months leading up to his murder – was also said to have been involved in discussions with the police over a contentious Eleventh Night bonfire, being built in the car park of the Avoniel leisure centre, further up the Albertbridge Road.[7] Police denied that any such discussions had taken place, saying only that officers may occasionally have bumped into the man in question along with others from the East Belfast Cultural Collective, set up expressly, in its own words, 'to offer advocacy support to isolated or smaller bonfires who have been targeted by statutory agencies... [and] feed into wider positive transition work ongoing within east Belfast.'[8]

There are strict rules governing bonfires – their placing and their composition (no tyres, no paramilitary emblems, no burning of symbols or images associated with the 'other side'). There are even grants, up to £1,750, for those bonfire-builders who adhere to (as most do) Belfast City Council's Good Relations Action Plan guidelines. The Avoniel bonfire, by its siting alone, infringed those guidelines. Staff at the leisure centre claimed to have been intimidated. (Staff at another east Belfast centre staged a walkout a number of years ago after threats from the UVF. I know this because it was the centre where my elder daughter went on a Saturday morning for ballet.) Contractors, who the previous year had been brought in to dismantle a large bonfire – at Cluan Place, as it happens – were warned off trying to stage a repeat. Graffiti went up: 'Masked Republican Mercenaries... Attack Loyalism at your own risk.' In contrast, a group of people of all ages and genders and numbering in the hundreds from the streets round about came out in support of the bonfire, joining hands in a chain around the base of the bonfire, saying that it was nothing at all to do with the UVF.

The argument runs that sectarianism has intensified in recent times, leading to an increase in the number of Orange parades as well as a literal bigging-up of bonfires, some of which can be several storeys high. I can't speak to the former but simple availability of materials, I would suggest, might have at least something to do with the latter. Which is to say, simple availability of wooden pallets. I was, as I said earlier, an enthusiastic bonfire-builder when I was growing up. Tyres we had back then – yes, though not many – and lots of odd bits of wood scavenged, donated (it was like an annual clear-out for some people), or hacked off whatever trees we could find and actually climb or reach into, but though we would have known a pallet if we had tripped over one, the fact is that we never did. Where they now come from and in such profusion is another question. Pallets, though, stack up in a certain fashion. And keep on stacking up and up and up and up. This is Jenga. Orangenga.

I have also heard the argument made that modern bonfire-building is an example of the engineering expertise that once went into shipbuilding – a bastion of working-class Protestantism – left with no other outlet once the yards went into decline, although that doesn't quite account for the fact that identical bonfires are to be found in nationalist and republican parts of Northern Ireland, notoriously under-represented (to the point of total exclusion in certain instances) in that industry. (It was one of the criticisms of the shipyard in its heyday that it employed very few Catholics.) The nearest equivalent to the Eleventh Night in republican areas is the Eighth (of August), the night before the anniversary of the introduction, in 1971, of internment without trial.

This year saw an almost identical situation to the Avoniel bonfire develop in the New Lodge area of north Belfast, where a bonfire had been built between three blocks of flats. Residents wanted the bonfire removed. Even the threats to local services were identical – 'our wood goes, this [community] centre goes' – and the threats to the contractors tasked with taking the bonfire down. The contractors were brought in under heavy police guard at 5 a.m. Both had to withdraw after two teenagers climbed to the top and refused to come down,* while police came under attack with bottles, bricks, fireworks and lengths of metal fencing.

Sinn Féin politicians were heckled and jeered by the bonfire-builders, whom the police said were being encouraged by dissident republicans. Carál Ní Chuilín, a former Culture Minister interviewed on Radio Ulster's evening news programme, ran through the things she and her Sinn Féin colleagues had brought to the area – the tens of thousands of pounds in investment – and sounded close to despair when asked what more could be done. 'I don't know.'

As with the DUP, there is much I would criticize Sinn Féin for, but my heart went out.

And then I thought, what about getting back into government?

After her father's murder, Ian Ogle's daughter said that he had been living with the expectation of an attack ever since his son had got into a fight in a bar with men who claimed to

---

* They ordered a Deliveroo, which the police, unsurprisingly, refused to let through.

belong to the UVF. The UVF ordered him to turn up for a 'punishment by appointment'. His father wouldn't hear of it even though he knew that that was likely to make him, or his family, a target for further attack.

That 'appointment' recalls Sinéad O'Shea's *A Mother Brings Her Son to be Shot* and is a further stark reminder that both loyalist and republican paramilitaries have kept up an almost constant campaign of attacks against people in – what they would claim were – their own communities. On 11 April 2018 – the day after the celebrations marking the twentieth anniversary of the Good Friday Agreement, which included the granting of the Freedom of the City of Belfast to President Bill Clinton and Senator George Mitchell – the INLA took a twenty-year-old man onto a patch of waste ground in west Belfast and shot him four times in the arms and legs. A neighbour told how she was woken by his screams.

Punishments are like a pornification of the culture (*Forrest Hump… Intercourse with a Vampire… You've Got Male…*) … twentieth anniversary? We can do you a twenty-year-old, face down on waste ground, one in each ankle, one in each knee: bang, bang, bang, bang. Perhaps with a view to their future safety and wellbeing, the victims are left nameless in reports, but all too often this leaves them voiceless too. One victim, though, spoke to *The Irish News*, describing how he was shot in his own home after he was approached on the street by men who threatened him and his father:

It shouldn't be allowed because there's bigger scumbags out there than me, I don't even leave the house… there's

bigger scumbags out there and they're not getting shot...
It's disgusting what they can do, disgusting that they can
just walk around and do it, they need took off the streets...
I seen it all and haven't slept, I'm wakening up seeing it all,
seeing the flashes. I'm turning around and seeing the gun
flashing, shooting at me and the big bang... I need to get out
of this area... I'm scared to even live now in my own house,
it's terrifying... They wreck your head, I don't know what
they have done to me, I'm just terrified, sometimes I don't
even want to live.

Of all the labels you could attach to them, the organizations
responsible for such attacks resent and refute 'terrorist'. However they choose to see themselves, though, it is impossible
to read that account without thinking that they do a pretty
efficient job of terrorizing.

Brutalizing too: a matter of weeks after they had murdered
Lyra McKee, republican paramilitaries in Creggan attacked
a teenage boy who was left with 'puncture-type wounds to
his shins' (bats with nails embedded in them are a favoured
weapon of paramilitaries of all hues). The uncomfortable truth
is that there is often more-than-tacit support for this sort of
paramilitary activity, usually on the basis that the police 'do
nothing'. Figures released on 12 March 2018 showed a 60 per
cent rise in such attacks over four years, from 67 to 101, or
around two a week. Loyalists appeared to reach first for the
bats and iron bars, republicans for the guns. (Figures in August
2019 say 81, up from 79 the year before and with 12 in June
alone.)[9]

The paramilitaries' charge sheets are notoriously catch-all – 'antisocial behaviour' is the grotesquely inapt term most often invoked to justify maiming. Sometimes the very fact that a person is beaten or shot stands as evidence that they must have had it coming. Sometimes getting the better of a paramilitary or the friend of a paramilitary in a fight or otherwise crossing one is all the victim needs to stand accused of. Or as the mother in Sinéad O'Shea's film says of her son, threatened with a second shooting, 'just being an ass'.

Liam Kennedy, one of the most assiduous campaigners against punishment attacks, calls them 'an astonishing toll of human suffering, directed particularly at young, working-class males, from loyalist and republican areas' and reckons that the 6,000-plus recorded instances from 1973 to 2013 is a gross underestimate.[10] Research carried out by academics from Queen's University puts forward a figure of 4,000 since 1998 alone. The Northern Ireland Commissioner for Children and Young People refers to those beatings inflicted on people under the age of eighteen as simply 'child abuse by armed groups'.

The maimers' argument runs 'because this is an abnormal society, we have to shoot young people in the arms and legs', not, as might be thought, 'this is an abnormal society because we shoot young people in the arms and legs'. (And an hour after writing that, I hear that two more boys – aged sixteen and seventeen – have been beaten in Derry. Police say the men who beat them used a crowbar.)

Of the world, basically, a piss-take.

★

Lyra McKee's funeral took place on the afternoon of Wednesday, 24 April, in St Anne's Cathedral, Donegall Street, long the starting point for protests and demonstrations that go out on to Royal Avenue and along the half mile to City Hall (I think particularly of one in support of marriage equality in June 2015, possibly the largest I have ever been on). As a teenager on a journalism training scheme, she had herself filmed across the road from the cathedral. 'I know now what I want to do with my life,' she said. A sentence that in the circumstances took on the most tragic irony.

The word had gone out in advance: mourners were encouraged to wear anything related to Harry Potter – Lyra used to joke about how she resembled J. K. Rowling's hero – or Marvel comics. (I only found out as I was about to leave the house. I attached two black 'bird-on-a-wire' clothes pegs to the lapel of my suit. If anyone asked me what they were for I'd say, 'This damn invisibility cloak. I took it to the dry-cleaners, and now look.') There were Hufflepuff and Gryffindor scarves aplenty, Superhero T-shirts inside and outside the cathedral – because hundreds of people had gathered on the street to pay their respects.

The Prime Minister was there, as was the Taoiseach and his Tánaiste, the Leader of the Opposition, the Secretary of State and the leaders of all the main Northern Ireland political parties, who, on the evening of the day after Lyra McKee was murdered, Good Friday, attended a rally in Creggan to express their outrage at her death and their condemnation of her killers.

Though the Dean of St Anne's led the service – with

contributions from Lyra McKee's sister and a close friend – the most electrifying moment came when he invited Fr Martin Magill, parish priest of St John the Evangelist on the Falls Road, and another friend of Lyra's, to address the congregation. (Fr Magill is also a member of the Stop Attacks Forum, which campaigns to end punishment attacks. The Forum's logo, with a black handprint at the centre of the 'O' of STOP, recalls the red hands left by the friends of Lyra McKee on the wall of Junior McDaid House.)

Given the opportunity to speak, Fr Magill didn't miss and hit the wall. Addressing the leaders of the Northern Irish parties directly, he welcomed the sight of them standing shoulder to shoulder the previous Friday, and then a moment later asked, 'Why in god's name did it take the death of a twenty-nine-year-old woman with her whole life ahead of her to make you do it...?'

The question might have been asked any time in the previous fifty years. Approximately half of all people killed in the Troubles were aged twenty-nine or under. More than one commentator in the immediate aftermath of Lyra McKee's murder picked up on the fact that she was the same age as Joanne Mathers was when she too was murdered in April 1981. Mathers, who was the mother of a two-year-old son, had been collecting censuses in Gobnascale in Derry's Waterside. An IRA gunman pulled her clipboard from her hand as she stood talking to a householder and shot her in the head at point-blank range. One of the most arresting of these comments came from Anthony McIntyre – a former member of the Provisional IRA turned critic of Sinn Féin:

Our IRA had no more right to shoot dead twenty-nine-year-old Joanne Mathers than their IRA had to shoot dead twenty-nine-year-old Lyra McKee… The fate of Lyra McKee, a personal friend, is not the first time I have had cause to reflect that we rose up to right a wrong and in the course of righting that wrong we violated too many rights ourselves. We did more harm than good.

Interviewed after Martin McGuinness had announced he was to retire from political life, Lowry Mathers, Joanne Mathers's husband, said – foreshadowing Fr Martin Magill – 'Joanne had her whole life ahead of her, but she was not lucky enough to live to retirement.'

None of which made Fr Magill putting his question to the politicians there in St Anne's any less powerful. It was, in fact, a brilliant bit of rhetorical and dramatic timing – catch them with the criticism while they are still smiling (self-deprecatingly, you understand) at the compliment you paid them. Almost as soon as the words were out, the applause started and the congregation rose to their feet. I had been sitting (and now like everyone else was standing) towards the rear of the nave, so it was only later, watching the news coverage, that I saw what had happened up at the front.

There, for two, maybe three, seconds, are the politicians still in their seats as, behind them, the entire congregation stands and applauds the priest who has just called them out. The look on their faces as the penny drops – *they aren't clapping for you: they are clapping against you*… you would like to think the feeling that must have accompanied it is one they will not soon forget.

Scundered.

You can find reasons enough to be cynical here sprouting on the surface without having to go digging around for more. When the Secretary of State and the Tánaiste announced just a few days later the resumption of talks, some commentators suggested that the minds of a few at least of our politicians might be concentrated by more than just Martin Magill's lambasting. For instance, the poor showing by Sinn Féin in local and European elections in the South – and the North – and the dramatic rise in support for the Alliance up here. Even the Open Golf Championship due to start in Portrush a fortnight after the scheduled end of talks may have played a part. So many eyes trained on us, so much dysfunction on display... so better at least look like we are trying to do something about it.

'But maybe,' I wrote in my notebook, 'politicians of all stripes here retain a residual sense of public as well as party obligation.'

Looking at this from the vantage point of late August I feel a bit like Charlie Brown, lying on the ground wondering where the ball went, again.

Cupar Street

In a famous study (well, it's famous here) first published in 1968 on the eve of the Troubles, the geographer Frederick Boal looked in depth at what he called 'Territoriality on the Shankill–Falls Divide'. Acknowledging in his introduction that 'segregation, on the basis of both economic and ethnic characteristics, is a feature of most cities' and considering such questions as surnames, morning newspaper of choice (traditionally the *News Letter* for Protestants, the *Irish News* for Catholics), he observed that 'The two areas [met] in a very narrow band which is almost entirely restricted to one street (Cupar Street).'*

When intercommunal violence broke out in August of the following year, Cupar Street, and the streets running off it, became the front line, and when the smoke of burning houses finally cleared, the first of the so-called peace lines appeared – rolls of barbed war or improvised barricades that later quickly hardened into peace walls.

* My mum, when she got her first job in the early 1950s, would cycle from the city centre, up the Falls, on to Northumberland Street, just down from Cupar Street, and from there on to the Shankill at the upper end of which she was then living.

The *Observer* newspaper, January 2012: 'The biggest peace wall in Belfast runs along Cupar Way.' (As with many of the – formerly – through streets in the area, Cupar Street was not only walled but truncated.) 'It divides the east Belfast loyalist area of Shankill Road from the Catholic Springfield/Falls Roads area of west Belfast.'[1]

In fact, the Shankill Road extends further west than the most westerly part of the Falls Road and lies slightly north of both it and the Springfield. Your East/West error (if Springfield/Falls Roads being Catholic are west, then the Shankill Road, being Protestant, must be east) is clearly infected by the Berlin Wall analogy or perhaps by the scene in Jim Sheridan's 1997 film *The Boxer*, in which Emily Watson as Maggie (no known surname) has her ID checked as she passes (under the watchful presence of a machine-gun post, and within sight of a Second World War-vintage staff car – on its way possibly to another film) a sign that reads 'You are now entering East Belfast'.

Daniel Day-Lewis as Danny Flynn awaits her on the other side: the wrong side for both of them, but sometimes love makes you do crazy things. 'I'm not sure about this, Maggie,' he tells her. To which Maggie says, with a half-smile, 'It's safer than being seen in West Belfast.' Clearly, it didn't occur to either of them to meet where the rest of us met, whatever side of town we were from, right in the city centre. (As with most films set in Belfast up to that point, the greater part of it was shot elsewhere, in this case Dublin... northside, not south.)

Belfast's is not a neat east–west divide.

The reality of division is a lot more complicated, and pernicious, with fences and walls forming internal borders between western neighbourhoods, northern neighbourhoods, eastern neighbourhoods. (In the south of the city not so much, though there are clear divides here too.) You can, in fact, see one of the peace lines as you come out of the Central (now Lanyon Place) Railway Station and look to your right, where the Albert Bridge levels out into the four-lane-wide Albertbridge Road. That advertising hoarding you can see on the left, just beyond the second set of traffic lights? The corrugated iron topped with mesh between that and the Credit Union building? Peace line. Cluan Place just beyond, in fact. If you have the time, take an hour or two and keep your eyes trained on that spot. Count on your fingers how many people walk from the Catholic Short Strand up the Albertbridge or vice versa. I am willing to bet you will not make it on to your second hand.

Land borders are curious. Unless defined by a geographical feature – river, mountain range – they most often run between peoples who, broadly speaking, have more in common with one another than either has with their respective capitals. They might appear necessary, or desirable, when you are far away from them – London, say – but get closer and it's hard to see where or why you'd draw the line. Belfast's peace lines are the exact opposite: the further you get from them, the easier it is to think they could easily disappear. Cluan Place, where Ian Ogle lived and died, is not just dominated by its peace line, it is almost wholly defined by it: a couple of dozen houses, tucked in, almost out of sight, between a busy main road and a redbrick wall – possibly the remnants of a factory – built out over the years to seal a former exit onto (or indeed entrance from) Short Strand, and all topped – to a total height of twenty-five or thirty feet – with that corrugated iron and mesh you can make out from Lanyon Place Station. A mural there details the violence that it has experienced: '5 People Shot, Houses Burnt, Houses Bombed, 20 People Intimidated Out by Sinn Féin/IRA'. Change the names of the organizations and other walls elsewhere in the city could tell similar stories.

Things have improved in recent years. As noted earlier in this book, elsewhere in Short Strand the 'peace line' takes the form of shrubbery and more or less discreet railings. (There is one small stretch of wall on which the word PEACE is spelled out in the cast face masks of local school children… adults now, they must be.) The difference between before and after the advent of the walls is that, before, there was regular traffic. Many of the recently created points of access and communication through the walls are still able to be closed at short notice.

As Belfast architect Ciaran Mackel has said, peace walls established a pattern of disconnection, not just between one neighbourhood and another, but – in their less aggressive (at least on first glance) form – between those (working-class) neighbourhoods and the centre of town. The Westlink dual carriageway, although first mooted before the Troubles (it was to be the Belfast Urban Motorway then – the BUM), became not so much a divide as a chasm. A chasm that, I would suggest, hiking up city centre rents from £20 to £30 a square foot will do nothing but widen.

Within those neighbourhoods – and again with security in mind (for which read policing) – the traditional row-houses were replaced with what was, in essence, according to Ciaran Mackel, 'suburban housing' in an inner city. Closes and cul-de-sacs, inward-looking and, unlike the houses they replaced, built of brick that bore no reference to the city itself. (Belfast brick, traditionally, was made of clay from Belfast's brickfields. A substantial part of Belfast literature is made from the contemplation of Belfast brick, of which *Belfast Confetti* by Ciaran Carson is the original and the best, not least the section called, simply, 'Brick'.)

Peace lines continued to grow in size and number, even after the signing of the Agreement in 1998. I am never quite sure how many there are at any given moment but I have heard, or read, figures ranging from sixty to ninety-seven in various parts of Northern Ireland, the vast majority in Belfast, and though there have been many admirable – and some successful – attempts to soften the look of them or find ways around, or through them, there is nothing to suggest that they will not be a fact of life here for many years to come.*

And because they have been erected in residential areas, like Cluan Place, off the main thoroughfares, it is possible, living here, to go for years without seeing some of them. Not long ago, in the making of a radio documentary, I walked for several hundred yards along the Shankill side of the wall at Cupar Way, far beyond the point where tourists these days gather. (More on them later.) Nothing has been done here to prettify

---

* James O'Leary from the Bartlett School of Architecture at University College London believes Belfast's walls are 'dematerializing slowly', which is not the same as coming down. He cites the example of Townsend Street, off the Shankill Road, where a 'palisade fence' was erected directly behind the old structure and then that old structure was taken down, moving the peace line a whole six inches to the left.

or otherwise finesse the wall into the surroundings. (Not, I should say, that I think prettifying and finessing are a solution to anything.)* In places, the roads that used to connect the different communities have not been entirely effaced: the kerb stones are still there, the expectation of uninterrupted passage. Almost more than the wall itself, these roads running into it and coming to a halt were what depressed me most. But I can say that. I don't live near it.

Back in 2013, I was involved – through a theatre company whose board I sat on – in a drama project, *The Conquest of Happiness*, inspired by the writings of Bertrand Russell. Described by the company, Prime Cut, as 'a dynamic combination of first-hand accounts and dramatizations of some of the most horrific acts of war of the twentieth and twenty-first centuries', the play was a co-production with a company from Bosnia-Herzegovina, East West Centar, and the Mladinsko Theatre of Slovenia. After opening in Derry – then the UK City of Culture – it was performed in Belfast, Sarajevo, Novi Sad and Mostar, cities all with their own recent experience of conflict.

As with Belfast, Derry does not divide along a simple, single line. Yes, the Waterside – to the east of the River Foyle – is sub-stantially unionist and Protestant, but there is a large housing estate there – Gobnascale – that is nationalist and Catholic. (My

---

* Recently released papers show that the Northern Ireland Tourist Board had suggested in the early 1990s landscaping the army watchtowers along the border, to take the bad look off the place. The papers do not say whether Alternative Arrangements of Ramsbottom, Lancashire, were ever asked to tender.

uncle, a police officer, was shot and wounded there in 1974 after travelling to a friend's house where I was staying to tell me not to tell anyone he was stationed in Derry. *Which I didn't know.**)

The Cityside (or Derry-side, indeed), across the river from Waterside, divides again between the old walled city and Bogside, though these days the bitterest divide is within, or immediately adjoining, the walls themselves, where a Protestant population that had once numbered in excess of fifteen thousand has dwindled to just over three thousand, about five hundred of whom live in the Fountain Estate.

In May of that same year, 2013, Peter Robinson and Martin McGuinness, incumbents of the Office of First and Deputy First Minister (OFMdFM), made a joint announcement, which Robinson described as probably the most ambitious set of proposals ever to have been brought forward in terms of a shared future, to dismantle all peace walls within ten years (that is, by 2023).[2]

It had been a central plank of *The Conquest of Happiness* that for the Derry performances, a section of the peace wall in the Cityside Fountain area would be removed. After months of talks, however, it became clear that the residents didn't want their wall to come down, no matter how temporarily. It was an indication of just how ambitious those OFMdFM proposals were and how largely unrealizable they would prove – or have to date proved – to be.[†] (In a bizarre footnote – or

---

* My uncle's name was John Patterson – Jackie. I have written about this at length elsewhere, but just to say here, he never fully recovered from the injuries he received that day. He committed suicide in 1988, aged 61.

† In fact, a newspaper report from the week of Martin McGuinness's death in

indeed parenthesis – to this production, the artistic director and general manager of Prime Cut were taken off a plane that was to fly them from Belfast on the first leg of the journey to Mostar. One of the job lot of denim jackets they had bought for the production was found to have a couple of live rounds of ammunition stitched into the lining.)

Segregation here is not, it should be said, only or even mainly characterized by peace walls, or confined to the cities: 80 per cent of all Housing Executive (public) estates are classified as 'single-community', this despite the fact that in a recent poll almost the same percentage of Northern Irish people said they would prefer to live in a religiously mixed neighbourhood.

If Cupar Street – with its tight-packed, late Victorian red-brick terraced houses – is the emblem of the August 1969 riots, then Springfield Park and August 1971 represents the next truly seismic rift in the city and its population. Built as the 1950s shaded into the 1960s, Springfield Park was a religiously mixed street of private semi-detached houses between the more distinctly Protestant Springmartin and Catholic Ballymurphy. It wasn't planned that way. As Frank Martin, who grew up there, says, people – most of whom would have come from the Shankill or the Falls – 'were just buying the best houses they could afford'. Within ten years of its completion, however, Springfield Park

---

March 2017 says that for the previous three years, there had been a Christmas market on the boundary between the nationalist and unionist communities and just a few days earlier a spring market to mark St Patrick's Day.

was literally caught in the middle of the violence that erupted following the introduction of internment without trial on 9 August 1971. The trailer for the excellent Northern Visions TV documentary *A Million Bricks* (directed by Frank Martin and Seamus Kelters, who had also grown up there) encapsulates the tragedy in the first twenty-five seconds of its commentary: 'After a night of violence in 1971, when six people were killed in the area, scores of Catholic and Protestant families were forced to leave their homes in one of the last mixed streets in west Belfast.'* This over footage of pairs of houses whose doors and windows have all been stopped up with cement blocks. (I was turning ten that August 1971 day in just such a house on the other side of the city.)

Even now, mixed housing developments can be – or feel – a little exposed. For the last couple of summers, the UVF has put up flags – or, one year, images of IRA atrocities – in a mixed development off Belfast's Ravenhill Road. After the first time it happened, four families moved out, despite a rare outbreak of unity among leaders of the then only recently suspended Assembly.

The Ravenhill development had been built as part of an Executive Office initiative known as 'Together: Building a United Community' (or T:BUC), a name as ugly as the aim is beautiful. 'Buck' when I was growing up was the equivalent in sense and taboo to 'fuck', and I can see our OFMdFM might not have cared for the sound of the abbreviated form of the

---

* All six were shot by members of the Parachute Regiment in the course of what has become known as the Ballymurphy Massacre.

more obvious 'Building a United Community Together', but already the language feels wrestled into submission by the task in hand, trying to reverse something that has been nearly half a century in the making.

At the time, the movements of population triggered by the summer 1969 riots in Belfast, and again by the violence of August 1971, were the largest since the end of the Second World War. That, of course, was before the partition of Cyprus in 1974, before the break-up of the Soviet Union, before the war in the former Yugoslavia.

In the last weekend of July, this third summer of Brexit, I found myself in conversation with a native of Mostar, now living in Rotterdam. We were at a conference in the Literarisches Colloquium Berlin (LCB) in the suburb of Wannsee. 'Rewriting the Map', as it was called, brought together artists and architects from Europe's divided cities: Mostar, Nicosia, Belfast and Berlin itself. It is tempting to put 'formerly divided' before Berlin, but most Berliners I speak to are adamant that thirty years after the Wall came down, their city is still divided into an (impoverished) East and (wealthier) West with Mitte (stag-and-hen-party-central) in between.

The father of the woman I was talking to in Berlin had been held in a concentration camp for three months during the war in Bosnia. On his release he was told that he and his family had twenty-four hours to get out: a very Belfast-sounding sentence, that, as was the one that came next. 'We just had the wrong surname. We didn't even own a Koran.'

One of her compatriots – the founder of a literary festival back in Mostar – was cynical about the premise of the whole enterprise: designed to milk funding, was his verdict. 'Always Mostar, Berlin, Nicosia and Belfast,' he said. 'It's like a pity-fuck.' Division is great for business, he said, several times in the course of the first conversation I had with him. Noticing the backdrop of the open-air stage where the conference's evening readings were taking place, he said, 'That is the Mostar Bridge.' The *Stari Most*, he meant, the sixteenth-century bridge, that is, blown up at the height of the war and dividing the town into a Bosniak east and Croat west, and since rebuilt. He sighed. 'I am starting to get a bit sick of it.'

A theatre company performs a piece that involves them emerging from the waters of the Wannsee, walking, dripping wet, up the long, sloping lawn of the LCB, mingling with the delegates watching on the terrace, repeating the words 'peace wall' and asking – the delegates? themselves? – 'Do you belong here?' They start tossing a brick between them – people instinctively move back – I have a long history of trouble with bricks and am not surprised when they finally set it right between my feet, before going inside and wrapping themselves in brown paper, emerging again to unravel a ball of red wool, which leads them finally out another door, across the terrace, down the long, sloping lawn, shedding clothes as they go, and getting back into the waters of the Wannsee.

The Mostar cynic asked, over my shoulder, where else but Berlin would you get money for something like this. I would be lying if I said there hadn't been times when I wondered myself about accepting invitations to such events. How do you, in all conscience, stand before a roomful of people in Hiroshima, say, and talk about the tragedy of your city?

But whether it was the particular historical moment or the combination of people that the organizers of 'Rewriting the Map' had brought to Wannsee, I had a very welcome sense of something new being said. If ever there was a moment to listen (and I was there, above all, to listen) to people who had seen their worlds overtaken, at bewildering speed, by division, it is surely now. And to listen too to what they have to say about trying to repair that damage.

Belfast is, as I said, a city of complex and pernicious divisions, but even in its worst times it was not, in the way that Berlin and Mostar were, a completely divided city, or in the way that Nicosia still is.

The Turkish Cypriot poet Neşe Yaşın described how, when she decided to travel to the Greek side, she had to take three planes: northern Nicosia to Istanbul, Istanbul to Limassol, Limassol to southern Nicosia, 'the longest 50m in the world'. (Though the divisions are nothing like as hard, it is true that in Belfast too the shortest distances are often the hardest ones to travel: it was always easier to get on a bus into town to meet someone than walk down a street that has a wall with a gate at the end of it.)

There are currently only two mixed Greek-Turkish villages in all of Cyprus. The buffer zone in Nicosia contains within it the corpses of buildings and cars caught in the middle in the war of 1974. So completely was the city divided that a bi-communal plan to restore a common sewage system in 1978 was hailed as a major advance: the accompanying graphic showed two arms, bent at the elbow, extending underground and connecting in a handshake, directly beneath a cross-section of wall.

Sometimes good shit happens.

The first crossing opened in 2003, the second a couple of years later, though in between times a referendum on reunification (2004) returned a massive No vote in the Greek south, even though the Turkish north voted, not quite as massively, Yes. Just this July, Nicos Anastasiades and Mustafa Akıncı, the Greek Cypriot and Turkish Cypriot leaders, announced the interoperability of mobile phones across the island (and made the first call themselves, hopefully not both at the same moment). The photo of their handshake calls to mind the sewer CBM (Confidence Building Measure). In the ether and in the drains, then, progress. And on the ground...?

After forty-five years of the sort of discussions I thought we in Northern Ireland had cornered the market in,* they are close to an outcome: either reunification through bi-zonal, bi-communal federation, or continued separation. Turkish Cypriots are already considered to be EU citizens, even though they are not subject to EU law. Don't ask me how trade operates there.

We don't have anything in our diagnostic vocabulary to match the German *Mauerkrankheit* – 'wall sickness' – to describe the

---

* One of my favourite newspaper headlines – 'Deal Reached' – hooray! you think, but, wait, here comes the smaller print – 'for Northern Ireland power-sharing talks... [to begin again].' (*Guardian*)

condition of living with the fear and tension brought on by division, by the physical fact of the Berlin Wall itself. But I am reminded again of those statistics that Lyra McKee drew on for her 'Suicide of the Ceasefire Babies' essay, and of the evidence they point to of stress and depression being passed from one generation to the next.

Hers would have been an interesting voice in Berlin. At the end of 2017, Lyra McKee recorded a TEDx talk at Stormont (I wish I could say proceedings had to be interrupted for the recording to be made*) – a talk that again touched on suicides of young people (young LGBT people in particular) but a talk that encouraged difficult conversations between people of differing world views; a talk that finally spoke admiringly of a Free Presbyterian mother who had gone to a gay club to support her son (and had a cocktail while she was at it).[3]

Maybe the most important line in it is the one that says, of a friend who became Christian and told her that her being gay changed nothing between them, 'Accept him for what he is as he has accepted you.'

The question of – the need for – shared education came up, time after time, though Mili Đukić, another of the Mostar writers, sounded one note of caution: people who were in the same class at school often ended up in different armies

---

* If golf is a good walk spoiled, then the Parliament Buildings at Stormont might be a good tearoom disturbed – though not often – by outbreaks of politics.

during the war. Mostar used to be held up as a model city. Along with Sarajevo and Vukovar, it had the highest number of mixed marriages in former Yugoslavia and now, he says, all three cities are ruined.

'What is this telling us?' he asked. 'That we cannot be together.'

After the war in Bosnia, a policy referred to as 'Two Schools Under One Roof' was introduced and in some places persists: Croatian and Bosniak children (and in some three-under-one cases, Serbian children too) educated in separate parts of the same school building or even in the same building at staggered times through the day and in different languages – very particularly in different languages, as provided for in the Dayton Peace Accords that brought the war in Bosnia to an end after more than three and a half years. Writing about this policy on the online platform *Open Democracy*, Tea Hadžiristić says the 'Romantic era idea of the ineluctable link between nationhood and language re-emerged during the war.'

Speaking in 2010, Peter Robinson described our own segregated schools in Northern Ireland as a 'benign form of apartheid', which was 'fundamentally damaging' to society here: 'We cannot hope to move beyond our present community divisions while our young people are educated separately... Future generations will scarcely believe that such division and separation was common for so long.' He recommended setting up a commission, which in Northern Ireland can be like digging a very large hole, placing things inside it, then patting down the earth once you are finished. I never heard another word about it.

*

Back home again from Berlin, I hear an interesting contribution to this debate from Andrew McCracken, head of the
Communities Foundation of Northern Ireland, who thinks
there is a problem in our education system (our society as a
whole) that goes deeper than the 'Orange and Green' divide:

> 'There's two sets of integration problems, of challenges at
> school. One is the religious differentiation. The other is that
> broadly wealthy middle-class families get their kids into the
> grammar schools and the poor kids go to the non-selective
> schools. And with all respect for the people working really
> hard on the Protestant/Catholic issue, if you give me a
> thousand pounds to do something about those problems,
> I'd put it onto the class issue – the rich and poor issue –
> because it gets even less of a time in the spotlight.'[4]

*

Somewhere in the middle of that very civilized gathering in
Berlin, I had a dreadful sense of foreboding. Wars, I thought,
are only ever inevitable in retrospect.

The most vicious wars are between people who know each
other well. And another perhaps equally obvious thought:
many more people end up fighting (and doing things they never
imagined themselves capable of) in wars than ever wanted
them to start. All it takes is everyone doing precisely what they
shouldn't do at the same time. Another line comes back to
me from *No Stone Unturned*, Alex Gibney's film about the UVF

massacre at the Heights Bar in Loughinisland: 'You would never have doubted anyone around here,' one of the survivors said. 'To come to this community was unreal.' In the way that people of both religions got along, he meant.

I don't *think* that this current crisis is heading towards war but neither am I pinning my hopes any more on the belief that we are better than that by simple virtue of being us. I have taken to describing myself as an eternal optimist but temporary pessimist. All the same, there are days when I feel this could all end very badly indeed.

All through the middle part of August, to mark the fiftieth anniversary of the Troubles, they are re-running news reports on TV of the 1969 riots.

Reporters stand in present-day Belfast at recognized interfaces that were shown in those fifty-year-old reports as hastily erected barricades (an abandoned TV set wedged, incongruously, in one) or rolls of barbed wire. Of all the many voices from that long-ago time, the one that stays with me is that of Methodist minister Revd Eric Gallagher, standing on a street, loudhailer in hand, pleading with shipyard workers not to get involved in the violence, 'For God's sake, keep this community sane. For God's sake and your own sake, keep this community at peace.' (This was not a sectional appeal. *Community* then had yet to be split in two. Community then still meant all of us together, not your particular side.)

Later, in that 1969 report, interviewed in his church, he says of the events he has just witnessed, 'You can talk about buildings, you can talk about jobs… This thing is just beyond description. I can see a generation being blasted into bitterness.' More than one as it turned out.

In Derry, during that week of black-and-white repeats, they are re-running the riots themselves, with petrol bombs thrown over the city walls from the Bogside on three consecutive nights. The trigger now as it was back then in 1969: the annual Apprentice Boys parade, in which one of the bands, Clyde Valley Flute, sports the Parachute Regiment emblem and the letter F on their specially adapted uniforms.

The police tried to restrict the band, who claimed harassment. Derry residents complained that they were allowed to march at all. A police superintendent quoted in the *Irish Times* said, 'Regrettably we are dealing with two very upset and hurt communities that are disappointed in police actions.' Upset and hurt. Add anger and a dash of antagonism and you have this year's unappetising summer cocktail.

15 August. Another night, another bonfire, another potential 'hate' incident. Derry again. In pre-internment days, 15 August was the traditional bonfire night in nationalist areas, being the evening of the day of parades by the Ancient Order of Hibernians (the 'Hibs': think Orangemen, then turn all their collarettes and banners green) marking the Feast of the Assumption.

(I drove around Belfast this 15 August and didn't see a single bonfire. I was wondering as I drove – trying to imagine my way back to that, the start of my ninth year – what had become of the bonfires in August 1969. And whether anyone could find it in them that year to go out and celebrate – as every second person I saw in town this night was – their A-Level results.)

In Derry, the Feast of the Assumption bonfire has now been transformed into a Festival of Fire, as part of the Gasyard Wall Féile, which straddles the two big August dates, 9–15 August. It looks like (and is) a genuine attempt by the Derry City and Strabane District Council to take some of the potential heat (forgive me) out of the night.

But not everyone is opting in. The bonfire at the centre of the latest story resembles – could almost stand in for – the bonfires at Avoniel and New Lodge: a tapering tower of pallets, adorned with flags for burning – in this instance Ulster, UDA, Union Jack, Parachute Regiment, Israel – along with a placard, six or seven pallets high, saying Soldier F. A banner runs along the bottom tier: 'Free Derry Says No To State Terrorism'. Interviewed on Radio Ulster's *Good Morning Ulster* programme, Neil Jarman, Director of the Institute for Conflict Research, says that he thinks what we are seeing is an increase in tension both between communities and within them.

I think of Mili Đukić, the Mostar poet. Even now that the bridge is rebuilt, there is 'something wrong' in Mostar. 'If you are a visitor, you cannot feel it in the first couple of days or even weeks, but if you stay there you will feel it eventually.'

Responding to comments by John Bolton, the then US National Security Adviser, that the American administration would push a trade agreement with the UK to the front of the queue after

a member of the IRA, but that war is over now. The people responsible for last night's incident are clearly signalling that they want to resume or restart that war. Well, I deny their right to do that.' It was powerful, and important. And yet, as previously said, once you have asserted your own right, it is hard to persuade other people that they can't assert theirs.

It is not a question of 'a bad lot', or a couple of bad lots, wanting to take us back to the past; this is the present to which everything that we and the people we voted for have been doing, and not doing, has been leading us.

To anyone who tells me it's better than it was (especially anyone who doesn't live here), I would say, yes, it is, but it's nothing like as good as it could have been, or we thought it was going to be.

Yet.

Up to Two a Day

When the boats (and planes and coaches and trains) come in

A few months before the signing of the Good Friday Agreement, James Cameron's *Titanic* was launched on the world's cinema screens. At $200 million, the film famously cost between a third and two-fifths as much again as the *Titanic* itself to make. (The ship's £1.5 million budget would have bought you $7.5 million in 1911, or $120–$150 million in 1997 terms.)

Up until then, surprisingly few people outside Ireland knew that the liner of the title had been built in Belfast. (Though even in the film itself, you have to listen very carefully for the evidence: it occurs two-thirds of the way through – which is to say, nearly two hours in – when the ship's designer, Thomas Andrews, played by a Canadian, Victor Garber, tells a Second Officer, Lightoller, that the lifeboats were tested in Belfast with the weight of seventy men... though given our history of producing 'wee men' that might only have been fifty of some other, better-fed place's.) Those who did know – Belfast people, in the main – I always felt were inclined to keep quiet about it because, well, you know, *the fucking thing sank*. Intriguingly, though, the first 'Titanic Society' in the world turns out to be an Orange Lodge, formed a mere eight years after the sinking by workers from the same shipyard where the liner was built, its banner featuring none other than Thomas Andrews. None of which is to take away from the well-documented sectarianism in the yard itself (one of the most famous plays of the 1950s, *Over the Bridge* by Sam Thompson, was an insider's-eye view of the issue), but it points to reasons other than the mere giving of offence or triumphalism for wanting to come together and parade.

The Titanic Society walked (that is the preferred term) behind Fairhill Flute Band, from north Belfast, in the Somme Memorial parade on 1 July 2019 when another band's bass drummer left that burst bass-drum skin, evidence of his fervour (whether for the cause or simply for the sound of his own drumming), lying at the end of my street.

International interest in the ill-fated ship coincided with the final dramatic decline of actual shipbuilding in the yards where the *Titanic* had been built, Harland & Wolff. (No new ships have been completed since 2003.) A company that at its height in the 1940s had employed upwards of thirty thousand now had a core workforce of only a few hundred. Refits and repairs were the orders of the day, with a sideline in wind turbines.

There was a lot of real estate up for grabs. Over the next fifteen years, the area formerly known as Queen's Island (land reclaimed on the east bank of the river in the nineteenth century) became the Titanic Quarter, with, at the heart of it, a bespoke visitor centre, Titanic Belfast. The Harland & Wolff gantry cranes, Samson and Goliath, each standing over 300 feet tall and painted a deep yellow, became the symbols of the city. In 2003 they were declared scheduled monuments, meaning that consent was required before there could be any change to their make-up or use.

And all the while the workforce numbers tumbled. My dad, a former shipyard worker, went to Titanic Belfast on the day in spring 2012 the centre opened. He told me when I picked him up afterwards that he had seen ghosts: not in the exhibition, but outside, on the streets of the 'Island'. 'All those men who used to work here…,' he said and shook his head.

Harland & Wolff had always been known for innovation. The liner my dad had worked on, the *Canberra*, had many revolutionary features… and the bad fortune to be launched (in the spring of 1960) just as air travel was beginning to make the passenger ship obsolete in its then form. Even with the severely reduced workforce of the 2010s, there were still technical advances. When a contract came in for oilrig 'jackets', special piles had to be sunk into the ground to provide support at the three weight-bearing points. (Most of Belfast city centre is built on reclaimed land, and recently reclaimed at that… If you wanted to build a city like Belfast, in fact, you really oughtn't to build it in the place where Belfast is.) As the workers I talked to there told me, once those piles were in, the yard should have been well placed to bid for similar contracts in future. And then in the middle of July 2019 came word from the management that unless a new buyer came in in the next few weeks, Harland & Wolff would be forced into administration.

When, at the end of that month, Boris Johnson arrived in

Belfast as Prime Minister and Minister of the Union to meet the parties at Stormont, a delegation of the remaining 132 Harland & Wolff workers mounted a picket – alongside supporters of an Irish Language Act – calling for the yard to be renationalized ahead of the threatened closure. After all, wasn't there, you know, something supposed to be happening on 31 October? Something that might make you want to keep your options and – by extension – one of your historically most important shipyards open? (Unless of course you had already made a decision about its place and Northern Ireland's in your long-term plans.)

A leading DUP politician at Westminster – petitioned by the workers for support – tweeted that the party didn't have the government over a barrel. To which the workers' representative replied, 'Well why not?'

Within four years of its opening, meanwhile, Titanic Belfast had been named the world's leading tourist attraction (we were so used to failure we would have been surprised that anything in Northern Ireland could win even *Northern Ireland*'s leading tourist attraction). Around three-quarters of a million were passing through its doors every year, a good half of them from outside Northern Ireland. This was tourism on a scale never before experienced in Belfast. And there was more to come.

In the early 2000s, the Northern Ireland Film Commission, founded the same year that *Titanic* was released, turned a vast former shipyard Paint Hall, a couple of hundred yards from where Titanic Belfast was (at that point yet to be) built, into Europe's largest film studio. In 2010, an HBO series booked time there. The series – *Game of Thrones*, based on the fantasy novel sequence by George R. R. Martin – was an immediate success, attracting more films and TV series to shoot in the studio and on location around Northern Ireland. (Nowadays, not only can Belfast play Belfast in on-screen portrayals of itself, it can play any number of other cities, including the unnamed one in BBC1's *Line of Duty*, set in a 'plausible liminal city' that is, according to Mags L. Halliday, definitely 'not Cheam'.)

I used to have this... gag would be going too far... call it *line* at live events about there soon being rival Westeros and Stark murals on Belfast gable-ends. There were nearly as many actors in the cast as there were 'volunteers' in the UVF. There were as many in the writers' room as there were in the Irish People's Liberation Organization, a splinter group of the splinter group that was the Irish National Liberation Army. (Oh, how the audiences la–... smiled politely.) They even had their own *Wall*, for fuck sake.

And, lo, starting the week before Easter 2019 – and coinciding with each of the eighth and final season's six episodes – a series of stained glass 'windows' was unveiled leading from Belfast's City Hall, over the river, past Titanic Belfast to the gates of the Paint Hall Studio (now renamed Titanic Studios). Each window in the 'Glass of Thrones' trail featured a different house from the series. The White Walkers window featured 'glow-in-the-dark' eyes, an innovation I hope the UVF never adopt. Those twelve-foot high gunmen are scary enough.

What could not have been predicted was how badly the last season was received. Almost as soon as it was over, a petition had been got up online to have the entire thing reshot. From the vehemence of some of the comments – 'I unfortunately had to watch this shit to know it needs redoing…'; 'David Benioff and D. B. Weiss need to be doused with shit and cars' – hold on… *cars?* – 'so that they feel what we feel after season 8…'; 'Season 8 is shit and the fans deserve better than D & D's half assed shitshow' – I wouldn't have been at all surprised to hear that a couple of the stained-glass windows had been smashed. (Anyway, they are gone now, on tour, not our responsibility.)

Not all the publicity *Game of Thrones* has brought has been good publicity. Sophie Turner who played Sansa Stark said at the end of filming that she was glad to be leaving Northern Ireland because of its abortion laws (this at a time when actors in the US were calling for a boycott of the State of Georgia after its governor signed a 'heartbeat' bill into law). Let me rephrase that: Sophie Turner's comments *are* good publicity for all who care that 1,053 women from here had to travel to England or Wales in 2018 for terminations. That's three a day.

Game of Thrones has opened Northern Ireland up to tourism in a way that no other single thing has, by establishing a trail that takes in locations from Castleward on the shores of Strangford Lough in the southeast through to Portstewart in the northwest. This has coincided with a mammoth increase in the amount of cruise ship traffic. The first cruise ship to visit the city docked as recently as 1996. In summer 2019 there is one cruise ship coming in a day, sometimes more than one, with a combined passenger list of 4,000 and fifty coaches and who knows how many taxis waiting for them. A new dedicated cruise ship terminal opened in late July – the first on the whole island. And total cruise tourism is soon expected to rise to close to 300,000 a year.[1]

On a visit to Belfast for TitanCon,* towards the end of August (all in all, a tricky and taxing month for many in Northern Ireland), *Game of Thrones* creator – 'Father of Dragons' – George R. R. Martin warned, 'If people are being blown up and shot then tourism's going to go right in the toilet so you can't go back to that.' I don't care whether tourism is in the toilet or out, George R. R., but we can't go back to people being blown up or shot, period.

Earlier in the summer, I got an email from a friend over from the States with a group of students she was hoping I would meet. 'They'll have an hour on Sunday,' she wrote, 'between Titanic and Thrones.' Two of the new holy trinity of Belfast's tourism Ts. The third (hands up if you guessed) – Troubles – has just been named at Number Four in Tripadvisor's UK Travellers' Experiences 2019, the only one of the top six not in London (it's sandwiched between the Mayfair Chocolate Ecstasy Tour and the Harry Potter Walking Tour for Muggles). Game of Thrones is there at Number Ten. The Troubles one is actually a city-centre walking tour, with as much of an emphasis on the

---

* The TitanCon history reads like something that might have come from the Combined Loyalist Military Command: 'TitanCon originated as a collaboration between several different groups who joined together to reach a common goal. On one side was the Brotherhood Without Banners (BWB) who wanted to put on a fan convention for *Game of Thrones* in Belfast and on the other was Belfast SF/F society The Other Ones, including Logan Bruce from Studio NI, who wanted to put on a SF/F convention in Belfast. And on the third side – did I mention there are three sides? – was Arkham Gaming Centre and TableTopNorth who wanted to put on a gaming convention in Belfast.'

road to peace as the Troubles themselves. The Cupar Way peace wall appears on another Tripadvisor list – at Number Eighteen of 213 things to do in Belfast. It is worth noting that high on the same site's 'things to do in Mostar' are the Sniper Tower and a War Tour. In Nicosia, the recently opened Ledra Street Crossing Point, between north and south, south and north, is Number Eleven of 251 things to do. 'Dark Tourism' is not a wholly Belfast phenomenon.

By far and away the greater part of those who died in the Troubles were civilians, many killed in bombings or random, religiously motivated gun attacks often in bars and other places of public resort, and yet the majority of memorials and gardens of remembrance to be found around the city of Belfast in particular (and to be seen on these tours) are to members of the same paramilitary organizations – self-described 'combatants' – who carried out those attacks. There are statistics for the religion of victims, their age, gender, but I have found myself wondering lately how many people who were killed had had their hair done that day, or had bought something new to wear. It might tell us a different story that cuts across the things that otherwise are presumed to set them apart one from the other.

Before the ceasefires, in the absence of any real tourist infrastructure in Belfast, 'Black Taxi Tours' grew up – think London Hackney cabs, think Hugh Grant, only sharing with five people he has never met and won't in the final act meet again and marry – tours that tended to have a hint of Green or Orange depending on where you hailed them, even though they drove back and forth across the sectarian divide. They remain hugely popular.

Mark Carruthers, in the BBC Radio Ulster documentary 'Telling Troubles Tales', visited fully fledged IRA and UVF museums, complete with weaponry and uniforms. (I think it said uniforms and not just balaclavas.) The loyalists needed more persuading before they would let the BBC in to record. There is a sense within loyalism that its paramilitaries get a bad press. To which you would have to say, Ian Ogle?

Claims by such museums to address frankly the full story of the past tend not to extend to associations with criminality, which goes as much for the IRA – in all its manifestations – as for loyalists. Witness the Provisional IRA's post-ceasefire murders of Robert McCartney (beaten and stabbed in 2005, in a narrow street as far in one direction from Lanyon Place Station as Cluan Place is in the other) and Paul Quinn, who was lured to a farm on the southern side of the border and beaten so badly – and methodically – that every bone in his body was broken. 'Nothing left for us to fix,' was how a surgeon put it to Paul Quinn's parents. Conor Murphy, a Sinn Féin government minister at the time, accepted the 'solid assurance' of the IRA in South Armagh that their members were not involved. (The DUP, who had only recently gone into government with Sinn Féin, said there was no evidence of 'corporate' IRA responsibility.) Murphy said the victim was a criminal. His parents and the police on both sides of the border deny this. His mother says his 'crime' was to have had repeated run-ins with the son of a leading Provisional. 'When you are a son of one of them you can say what you like to anybody.'

Paul Quinn had already been told that he would be 'got along the side of a road in a black bag'. Twelve men were involved in the beating. Twelve more waited outside. You would need the side of the barn they carried out the murder in to paint them all into the mural. Disinfectant was used in the clean-up. Ra ways… To adapt the 1980s republican 'armalite and ballot-box' slogan, with a baseball bat in one hand and a bottle of Jeyes in the other, we will stay out of jail long enough to take power in Cullyhanna.*

In the early summer of 2018, I went down to the Titanic Quarter with my twelve-year-old daughter for BBC Radio 6 Music's 'Biggest Weekend'. I wish I could say the highlight of the day was Public Service Broadcasting performing their White Star Liner EP-length suite on the slipways where the *Titanic* was built, but I missed them altogether. It was my daughter's first proper gig. After a handful of sets – Courtney Barnett, the Breeders, Manic Street Preachers, the Orielles, David Holmes – her interest was on the wane. We checked out for a while and went for a ride on the Ferris wheel. We had the entire thing to ourselves, so when we reached the apex, the operator down

---

* Paul Quinn's native village and a Provisional IRA stronghold. Suzanne Breen, a Northern Ireland Journalist of the Year and current political editor of the *Belfast Telegraph*, wrote an account of the murder and the circumstances leading up to it for her previous newspaper, the *Sunday Tribune,* that includes the observation – telling in more ways than one – from one local resident, 'Diesel men don't kill diesel men. They might have the odd row about territory, but it's settled peacefully.'

below hit pause. May have had a cup of tea, for all I know, for we had all the time in the world, it felt like, to look about us.

I could see directly facing us the line of the Belfast hills, with Cave Hill jutting out like a ship's prow. I could see, closer at hand, between the hills, the city and right down the man-made Victoria Channel – whose construction in the 1820s was instrumental in Belfast's transformation from commercial town to industrial city – as far as the mouth of Belfast Lough. I could see, looking back towards the city a little way, beyond the Biggest Weekend stage, the spot where ten years before I had been persuaded to stand on a vast mound of rubble (apartments now) for a BBC documentary about the Titanic Quarter, while – in the broadcast version, and at my request – Woody Guthrie sang 'This Land is my Land' (I meant it as a challenge not a given). I could see, looking east, vast empty tracts of what had once been shipyard and was not yet whatever Phase 2 or 3 of the Titanic Quarter roll-out had in mind for it to be.

There was still work going on, though, around the base of the enormous cranes. They reminded me of great beasts whose habitat was gradually shrinking. It wasn't clear where there was left for them to go. And then I saw the flames. They were coming from a castle on the opposite side of the cleared land from the cranes. A long line of people was making its way out of the back of the castle in a very calm and orderly fashion. These were extras and that was the set of the final series of *Game of Thrones*. I thought about taking out my phone, trying to get a panorama shot, but then I thought, no, just take it in, commit it to memory. This is what this place is, May 2018.

My daughter shrieked with delight. 'Look down there!' I looked. I shrieked too. We were right above the men's outdoor toilets, multiple four-way urinals at which multiple men attempted to urinate while simultaneously drinking beer from plastic cups. And I thought, commit that to memory too, why not? Then the big wheel started turning again and we got to the bottom and I said to my daughter, what do you think, seen enough? And she said, yeah, seen enough, and off we went, back up the road, past the gates of Harland & Wolff.

The next time I was back there on foot was the beginning of August this year. The administrators had been called in. The workers were staging a round-the-clock picket. Belfast playwright Martin Lynch had been in touch with the Unite Union about arts workers coming down to show their support. It was a very last-minute arrangement. About half a dozen of us turned up on a Saturday morning. I admired the baseball caps the workers were wearing – all black with the Harland & Wolff logo – an H overlaid on a W – in thick yellow-gold thread, and below that the words 'Built in Belfast'.

At some point a microphone was produced and the Unite organizer asked us if we wanted to say a few words. I told the story about my dad and the *Canberra* and about visiting Titanic Belfast. He had died, I said, in the autumn of 2017 but I knew how proud he would have been of what they were doing. It was raining by this time. As I was leaving to walk through the Titanic Quarter into town, one of the men handed me his cap. 'For your Da,' he said.

★

The week after Harland & Wolff went into administration, the Scottish government announced that it was planning to nationalize the Ferguson shipyard in Glasgow after it too looked set for closure. (Nationalize it, in part, because EU competition rules prevented them from simply handing over a cheque for the money required to keep the yard open.)[2]

The contrast with the Belfast yard – with no government locally to appeal to – could not have been starker. Meanwhile, 1.7 million people have gone on to change.org to sign a petition demanding the reshoot of the final season of *Game of Thrones*. Elsewhere on the site, the petition calling for the renationalizing of Harland & Wolff has attracted 3,023.

3,024.

Save Our Shipyard.

Uppa Queers

On Culture Night 2015, I conducted a marriage ceremony on the steps of Belfast's Merchant Hotel between Malachai (Mal) O'Hara and Michael McCartan.

It was, if not a stunt, at least a pointed statement jointly organized by Amnesty International and the Belfast Rainbow Project, drawing attention to the fact that, following the Referendum earlier that year in the Republic of Ireland, Northern Ireland was now the only place on the islands where same-sex marriage was not recognized. Stunt, statement or pure performance, I had nevertheless thought it fitting that I got myself ordained for the occasion. Online. The American Marriage Ministries. It took me about fifteen minutes to fill in the application. 'Your application has been submitted to our Church Board. If this page does not refresh in thirty seconds...' But it did, and, lo, the Board in its ineffable wisdom had laid their virtual hands on me, and there I was, able to conduct marriages in forty-I-forget-how-many of the fifty states.

We performed the ceremony twice, to a rapturous response from a large audience that filled most of Waring Street, on which the Merchant stands, and each time the vows sounded to me as real as any vows needed to be.

We were not always so behind the curve here. Belfast City Hall conducted the first same-sex civil partnership in all of the UK, on 19 December 2005, between Grainne Close and Shannon Sickles (now Shannon Yee). Protestors from the Free Presbyterian Church hired an advertising trailer bearing the message, 'Repent ye therefore, and be converted.' One supporter of the married couple held up a placard to the protestors: 'The earth is flat.'[1]

Free Presbyterian pickets, of course, are something of a Northern Ireland cliché. Members of the church picketed an all-male production of *Romeo and Juliet*. (You can only think they'd have had their work cut out for them in Elizabethan England.) They picketed Gilbert and George, much to the artists' evident delight. (As Gilbert remembered, 'They were shouting "Sodom and Gomorrah". And George said, "Where is this club? When does it open?"')[2] Just as when we were in our teens we chose films according only to the Xs they were awarded (one picture house in east Belfast specialized in *double Xs*), I know people who wouldn't have considered going to see a production that hadn't drawn a picket.

The nadir came in 1977 with the 'Save Ulster From Sodomy' campaign, launched by Paisley – in his role as leader of the Free Presbyterian Church, rather than of the DUP, though in those years you could hardly have put a cigarette paper between the two. (They'd probably have confiscated your cigarette paper before you got anywhere near them.) The campaign was in direct response to the attempt by the Northern Ireland Gay Rights Association to challenge the government's refusal to extend the 1967 Sexual Offences Act, decriminalizing homosexuality for over-21s, to Northern Ireland and – all too easily forgotten – Scotland. Belfastman Jeff Dudgeon took a case to the European Court of Human Rights in Strasbourg, and won, in 1981, the year after homosexuality had been legalized in Scotland.

It's a long journey from Save Ulster From Sodomy to the election of the first openly gay DUP councillor. Or rather the nomination – since her eventual election was in the voters' hands. Baroness Paisley, as previously noted, was far from approving. Perhaps signalling a growing separation between the party that the Baroness's husband had founded and his church, Free Presbyterian John Greer railed against the DUP's decision to stand an 'out and out lesbian' (there's out, I guess, and then there's out and out) for a local council election at all. There was an agenda abroad, he said, that aimed to persuade 'the child of God' that things like sodomy were no longer wrong, adding mournfully, 'That's the type of thing that's going on in our own little land.' ('Our own little land' trades in the same currency as 'Our Wee Country', which for a time became synonymous with the Northern Ireland football team and went hand in hand with the chant 'we're not Brazil, we're Northern Ireland'. Not all the football fans I know approve: 'People here,' one friend said to me, 'need to raise their fucking expectations.')

In those same local elections that saw Alison Bennington returned, Mal O'Hara, now deputy leader of the Green Party and founder of Alternative Queer Ulster, was elected to Belfast City Council for the Castle ward, one of three LGBT councillors. (Three sitting LGBT councillors did, however, lose their seats, including Jeff Dudgeon – these days a member of the UUP – who had taken the landmark court case that led to the extension of the 1967 Act to Northern Ireland. That was then, this is now.)

Mal O'Hara turned up for his first council meeting in City Hall wearing a T-shirt with 'Uppa Queers' across the chest (that's 'Up The Queers' for the cloth-eared among you). It was a powerful moment – and message – of affirmation and change. An article he wrote for the Queen's University Sinn Féin society (though he was not a member himself) back in 2014 gives a flavour of the sort of new political thinking that may – for, as ever, it is best not to overstate here – just be beginning to take hold:

> [I'd like to see a] fairer, greener, socially just and more equal Ireland. Not ripping the North away from the UK and remodelling it to look like the South. This is much more radical than that. It is about creating a new vision of a new Ireland, not some bastardized version of the Celtic Tiger with the North shoved on.[3]

Mal O'Hara was the person I heard on TV, back in the spring, saying he had planned a civil partnership in the autumn (as had another good friend of mine) because he saw no imminent prospect of a change in the marriage laws.

It wasn't just the DUP that was blindsided by the 8 July Commons votes on abortion and marriage-equality reform.

Nobody saw it coming. I was (am) delighted but if I'm being honest, a little saddened all the same that we hadn't been able to get there – and sooner – on our own, not least to ward off any future challenges or judicial reviews. And, if I'm doubly honest, I am a little uncomfortable too celebrating a victory (long overdue) for something I believe in achieved by means which – if they were used to move legislation I was opposed to – would be a cause of consternation.

Mal O'Hara also sits on the board of Lighthouse, a north Belfast charity dedicated to helping those in danger of self-harm or suicide. Everywhere you turn here, you run into those suicide statistics, and more than statistics. At the start of last autumn, I decided to take a walk – I try to do it once a year – up Cave Hill. I chose a route I had never used before, which involved driving out of the city and coming at the hill from the far side. It's a remote spot. Within a minute of parking my car, I found myself on a path with, either side of me, trees, almost every one of which had a placard on it, urging all who read them not to despair, offering them numbers to ring, verses to read, places to go when hope is gone… And on four of those trees there are memorials to people who even those messages could not dissuade from ending their lives.

Philly O'Donnell, the son whose mother brought to be shot in Sinéad O'Shea's film, talks about his own feelings of bleakness, about thinking of 'throwing the rope up' and about a friend his own age (nineteen) who has 'jumped the bridge' in such a way that you know the sentences are part of the idiom.

We badly, badly need to start taking proper care of all our citizens.

★

The amendment to the constitution in the South to allow for same-sex marriage was passed by more than six in ten of the electorate, in a referendum in May 2015 – still to date the only place where the measure has been adopted by popular vote.

I will never forget taking the bus down to Dublin for an event the night after the referendum, falling asleep with my head against the window and awaking as we came into Dublin, and looking up and seeing rainbow flags fluttering from every lamppost and I thought of the old loyalist slogan, 'We will not swap the blue skies of Ulster for the grey skies of an Irish republic...'

Yeah, right.

Even for those of us who did not think of ourselves as unionist, still less loyalist, it had been one of the few comforting thoughts about growing up in Northern Ireland that at least we weren't living in the South, with all its clerical interference in matters of public morality. Those trains up to Belfast in the 1960s carrying women intent on buying condoms to bring back down to Dublin in defiance of the law. Those unhappy couples unable to get a divorce.

My first visit to Cork as a grown-up, in the early 1990s, was an eye-opener. (My only previous visit had been on a family holiday, in the summer of 1969. A woman in a shop my mum went into outraged her by tutting at the sound of her accent. 'What an awful place that is up there.') I shared a house for part of the time I was in the city with the director of the Lesbian and Gay Film Festival, whose programme seemed to pass off without picket or protest. In fact, in just a couple of years, it had become one of the highlights of the Cork cultural calendar.

I was still living there in the spring of 1994 when a junior government minister, Emmet Stagg, was found in his car with a man believed to be a prostitute. Labour Party colleagues rallied round, as did the Fianna Fáil leader of the coalition govern-ment, Albert Reynolds, who said it was a time for 'charity and restraint'. It was difficult to imagine such charity or restraint in Westminster, let alone in political institutions, such as they were in those pre-ceasefire days, in the North. As for the public, their anger seemed to be directed more towards the police officer who had leaked details of the incident to the press.

A friend I had made there explained to me (better I'm afraid than I am about to) that it was the sunny flipside of the Republic being a mono-religious state. Catholicism was so all-pervasive, he said, that most people just went along with it. 'Nodding terms' was the phrase he used. They would never dream of holding anyone to a higher standard than they would ever have held or wanted to be held to themselves.

I had already spent enough time in Dublin with other, younger writers for it not to have been a complete surprise to me that the South had developed in a very different way from the North, and not at all in a direction that either unionists or nationalists imagined. And one of the first things that was apparent was that – with a few conspicuous (and, it seemed at the time, not well-supported) exceptions – it wasn't really looking to the North at all.

I checked myself briefly, by the way, when I first wrote that sentence about how we used to feel more enlightened and liberated than the rest of the island: maybe that was just you, I thought. Two days later – it was Pride Week – I was on the Big Gay Tour of Belfast when one of my guides – Richard Orr – said exactly the same thing: 'The North used to look down its nose at how backward the South was… Not anymore. It's all been turned on its head. Now, we look *up* to *down there*, and wish.'

This was about three stops on in the tour from the Parliament on Corporation Street, for a long time Belfast's best-known gay nightspot. There in spring of 1997, a young RUC man, Darren Bradshaw, was shot dead on a night out. Richard Orr said he knew Darren Bradshaw to see – always stood in the same spot – which clearly whoever targeted him noticed too. The man who shot him – he was in the INLA – walked straight up behind him and pulled the trigger. 'I tell you all this,' Richard Orr said, 'in case you think it was some sort of utopia then, divorced from everything else that was going on. It wasn't.'

The *Lost Lives* entry for Darren Bradshaw's murder quotes an LGBT member of the Irish Republican Socialist Party, the INLA's political wing: 'I have no problem with the attack. He was a member of the RUC. He put on a police uniform and became part of a state that oppresses nationalists. His sexuality is irrelevant.'

Which, in a way, it was. His humanity was not.

A couple of years later, the first purpose-built gay nightclub in Northern Ireland – the Kremlin – opened its doors and hung out the rainbow flags. Richard Orr again: 'It's not tucked away or trying not to draw attention to itself…' It's about this point in the tour that a car passes and toots its horn, the driver shouting a greeting out the window to Richard and our other guide, Donal Kelly. 'That's Paul,' Donal says, 'taxi driver.' And then Richard tells me that Paul met his wife at a riot. 'On the same side?' I ask. 'No, it was real love across the barricades. They used to wait until the Boys had gone home' – the Boys who orchestrated things, he means, on both sides – 'and then they'd shout out to each other. They met again later on Bebo.' Bebo sounds more archaic to my 2019 ears than riots, alas. 'Actually, he was one of the kids in the Zombie video.'

'The *Cranberries*?'

'Yeah. Was paid a couple of packets of fags.'

The video (I watch it as soon as I get home) shifts between black and white and colour, between a Belfast where troops patrol and filthy-faced boys play in derelict buildings, and a studio where other boys, sprayed all-over gold (I wish I could say the same boys, a day out at least to go with the couple of packets of fags), sit at the foot of a cross where Cranberries singer Dolores O'Riordan (gold too, head to toe) stands and sings the words she wrote after the IRA left bombs in litter bins in Warrington, in Cheshire, in 1993, killing two young boys.

The BBC wouldn't screen it when the song was first released, but it's a time capsule now – the troops long gone, the fortifications around the base they emerge from, the derelict buildings, Dolores O'Riordan herself... And as for the song itself: that too to my 2019 ears doesn't sound as overwrought as it once did. 'In your head... in your head... they are fighting...'

Donal Kelly shows us a photo of one of the earliest Pride marches. The very first one – in 1991 – attracted about a hundred people. There can't be that many more in the photo

Donal shows me, though what really catches my eye – what helps me in the end to date it (1996) – is the billboard the parade is passing in front of, a poster on it for the latest Tom Cruise movie: *Expect the Impossible* the tag line runs.

I don't know how many of those marching in the mid-1990s could ever have expected nearly 60,000 people turning out for Pride less than a quarter of a century later, with serving members of the police among the marchers, though it is still, thanks to our Parades Commission, one of the most heavily policed and regulated Pride parades in the world (according to Richard Orr). And Northern Ireland still – despite all the advances – has the worst record in Western Europe for homophobic attacks. I put a question mark next to this in my notebook – not because I doubt my guides, but because the worst/best/most/least are the kind of thing we all occasionally say too readily. But the very next morning I am reading a report on the BBC news website that there has indeed been a nearly 25 per cent increase in homophobic crimes (up from 163 to 201) in the past twelve months. (Though this is, admittedly, in a sidebar to an interview with a young woman saying she has never experienced any prejudice at all. Her granny, in fact, was almost desperate for her to come out to her.[4])

Pride this year fell on the same wet August Saturday afternoon that I stopped off to see the Harland & Wolff workers. The Unite rep had told me to wear my cap if I was going into town to watch: the union had a big contingent marching who would be delighted to see it. I didn't want to say I felt a little shame-faced: I was touched on my dad's behalf to have the cap but I had done nothing myself to earn the right to wear it.

Crossing over the river (where poor Emily Watson had once to submit to ID checks) to the eastern edge of the city centre, Custom House Square, all I could see were rainbows. People and rainbows. (It pleased me no end to see that a guy who looked and sounded like the guy who used to sell – and call out – three lighters for a pound and ten sheets of 'wrapping-up paper' for fifty pence was selling tiny plastic rainbow flags.)

The parade was still forming up but the footpaths were already thick with spectators, as dressed for the occasion as the people they had come to watch. I admired, in passing, one woman's rainbow umbrella and for the second time in half an hour was given a thing as a gift. I tried to refuse but it was OK, she told me, they were only cheap things, out of Dunne's Stores. 'And, look,' she said, 'we have another.' 'We' being the other man and woman with her. They were up from the South for the day, up for our Pride. 'Just to see it.'

I had decided that the best place to watch from was the bottom of Donegall Place, where the street (the city's main shopping street) meets Donegall Square – the City Hall directly facing – and where the parade, more than halfway through its route by that stage, would take a turn to the left on its way back to where it began.

It being a Saturday lunchtime, there were a dozen or so – mostly men – gathered at the gates of City Hall (from which today the Rainbow Flag was flying for the first time) with Union Jacks and banners, still protesting, as they had been for more than six years, the decision to fly the flag of the UK only on designated days. There was, a few yards along from them, a group of evangelicals in singing and testifying mode – again this being a Saturday, although their numbers this week were perhaps swollen not *with* Pride, but in reaction to it.

I could see, over the tops of the heads of the people gathered to watch the parade, placards reminding us all (again) of the precise Old Testament lines in which God tells people not to love each other if they are man and man or woman and woman and if they fear everlasting damnation. And then a few minutes later, the floats started coming down Donegall Place (Christians At Pride far outnumbered the crew at the City Hall gates) and the Dixie Cups' 'Chapel of Love' drowned out the hymns: 'Goin' to the chapel and we're going to get married'. That might have been a touch premature but it seems almost certain now that they are – those who want to – going to get married, here in their own city.

The rain was coming down even heavier now. No matter what way I turned my umbrella, rain kept running off onto two women standing to my right and a little behind me. In the end, the obvious solution was to give the umbrella to them. I put the Harland & Wolff cap on. I waved to the Unite marchers. So did about a hundred other people standing around me. I doubt very much they saw me.

Leo Varadkar, the Irish Taoiseach, got a huge cheer as he passed, as did the (very substantial) Sinn Féin contingent. The SDLP got a decent response. The UUP's group was past before anyone around me had recognized them or parsed their Pride in the Union rainbow Union Jacks. (All their quartered crosses-saltire and counter-charged argents and gules.) At least they were there though. (And their flags were pretty.) The DUP – shit to have to say 'needless to say' – were not.

Coming in in second place, meanwhile, in the political party cheers stakes – though it was a close-run thing between them and the Greens and People Before Profit – was the Alliance Party.

A survey earlier in the summer suggested that, for the first time ever, more than 50 per cent of people here saw themselves as neither nationalist nor unionist.

This was interpreted by some as worse news for unionism, the feeling being that 'neithers' were more likely to be Protestants alienated by the DUP especially. The figures bore out what the most recent elections suggested, that there has been a growth in support for the Greens, People Before Profit and especially Alliance. (In Northern Ireland Assembly designation terms, to say again, all three declare themselves not as 'neither' but other.) Alliance are still, just, the fifth largest party in the Assembly and at local councils, although they are within touching distance of the SDLP and not all that far behind the UUP. In terms of votes for the European Parliament, however, they are third, more than doubling their vote between 2014 and 2019. For once the 'surge' does not seem like hyperbole.

(It is tempting to say that Brexit itself has helped unleash something new in Northern Irish politics but I sense – without attributing to this a rise in support for any one party – Lyra McKee's murder too has played a part. It is not that younger people were uninterested in politics before – they were, passionately, just not in our politics. My elder daughter had an Instagram blog in her early teens with 15,000 followers – probably more than all the adult bloggers I knew put together. She commented on everything and everywhere under the sun... except here. The world was her donut. Northern Ireland was the hole. I ask her now whether she and her friends are talking about the political situation here. She looks at me as though I am insane. Of course, she says.)

Belfast writer Jan Carson gently lampoons the 'nice', squeamish-Protestant image of traditional Alliance voter in her story 'Filters':

> Tim and her have always voted Alliance. They don't really concern themselves with the ins and outs of Alliance policy. It's enough to know they are supporting the middle ground; a party that is neither us nor them. They think of themselves as progressive Protestants; tolerant and open to change.

Conor Cruise O'Brien – the Dublin-born Irish Labour Party government minister who made the unlikely transition to UK Unionist Party member of the Northern Ireland Forum in the run-up to the Good Friday Agreement – once described Alliance as unionist where the 'u' was so small they were practically *nionist*. There has always, though, been a bit more to the party than that. Anna Lo, the first Chinese-born person elected member of a national assembly anywhere in Europe, was an Alliance representative for more than ten years on Belfast City Council, as well as at Stormont. She left politics, finally, when she became the target for racial abuse following that Council decision to limit the number of days on which the Union Jack flew from the City Hall – abuse that went up still another notch when she expressed a preference for Irish reunification.*

And still Pride was passing, in the rain, the front of the City Hall. There was one more resounding cheer, where I was standing, for the PSNI. The officers marching looked delighted – as did the two people in Garda uniforms marching with them. Stupidly, I felt myself starting to cry.

Like Pride the world over, there is something a little corporate-looking about some of the floats and banners, but there is still room for individual expression. One of the smaller, handwritten, placards reads 'Fuck the DUP', another simply, 'We're Winning – Uppa Queers!'

And later that night, two women walking home together from Pride were attacked and beaten in east Belfast.

In July 2019, in her first significant vote as an elected representative, Alison Bennington sided with her DUP colleagues on Antrim and Newtownabbey Council in opposing the flying of the rainbow flag from Council buildings during Pride celebrations. The motion passed anyway, as perhaps she all along knew it would, with the support of Alliance, SDLP, Sinn Féin and Ulster Unionists, voting (as the UUP allows) with their conscience. Even so, she got some stick. Part of me finds it hard to get too worked up. Choose your battles. She's there. *Out* and there. And in the DUP.

---

* In an interview with the *Belfast Telegraph* in 2016, she was quoted as saying she said racism was more extensive and vicious than when she first arrived in Belfast in 1974.

Up and Down
the Road

Hong Kong in the Irish Sea

I'm out on the main road near my house, doing a bit of shopping. One shopkeeper friend asks me what I'm up to these days. I tell him, this book. He shakes his head. 'I voted Remain,' he tells me, 'would have been an enthusiastic Remainer, but...' his expression is pained – it's upsetting him to say this, or even think it – 'I see people in here, they didn't vote Leave because they're stupid.'

It's something I have been thinking a lot myself. I am European to the core but this bears repeating: it is all right to want to leave the EU, as it is all right to want to leave any political arrangement, of which in the course of human history there have been many and of which, in the centuries and millennia we will not be here to witness, there will be many, many more. If you are going to leave anything, in fact, voting seems far from the worst way to go about it.

Forcing a departure, on terms – which is to say, no terms

– that a majority of the population did not specifically endorse, though, that is, always, going to be a different matter.

'After a period of relative obscurity, it now appears that everybody is fascinated by the Border. It is interesting, for a while, to be the centre of the world's attention, but I think on the whole many of us would rather have been left alone.'

It reads like a post on the @IrishBorder twitter feed but, in fact, it is an extract from a letter by John McDowell, the ('arch', I'm tempted to say) Bishop of Clogher, to Prime Minister Boris Johnson on his third day in Downing Street. 'No Government,' the letter goes on, 'should commit a country to a course of action in which the consequences were so opaque as to be incalculable.'

He didn't receive a reply.

Asked by the *Belfast Telegraph* why he had written it, the Bishop said, 'the fact is that English ministrations and people in important positions in England are very detached from reality in Northern Ireland. I don't think they understand it.'[1]

Perhaps he had in mind another of those who had been in the running for the Conservative Party leadership, Dominic Raab, who claimed in an interview to have 'walked the border from Newry to Crossmaglen'. Leaving aside for a moment that the border doesn't run from Newry to Crossmaglen, this is a distance of some fifteen or sixteen miles. The border is 310. (His calculations would have been made vastly easier had Margaret Thatcher's wish come true. According to her former private secretary, 'she thought that if we had a straight line border, not one with all those kinks and wiggles in it, it would be easier to defend.'*[2]

Writing in the *Irish Times*, meanwhile, before the result of the Tory leadership contest was confirmed, Katy Hayward, Senior Fellow in the 'UK in a Changing Europe' initiative, had a similar take on London's poor grasp of Northern Ireland realities:

> The two remaining candidates for British prime minister describe no-deal Brexit as if it were akin to an unsightly war wound they'd personally bear with brave nobility... In an environment of such existential uncertainty, the provision of facts and analysis plays both a guiding and a sobering role.[3]

Full Fact, the UK's Independent Factchecking Charity, puts the figure for goods and services travelling north to south at £4 billion in 2016, and goods travelling south to north (no figures being available for services) at £1.3 billion.[4] A leaked May-era memo suggests that the agricultural element of this could virtually stop in the first twenty-four hours after a no-deal Brexit, while all other trade would significantly slow.†

(DUP support has traditionally been strongest on the eastern side of Northern Ireland – counties Antrim and Down – with

---

* Raab spoke in the same interview about livestock checks already in place in the County Antrim port of 'Learn', prompting one social media wag to ask would English politicians never 'Larne'.
† It didn't find its way out until the start of August. There are so many leaks at the minute they are operating on a ticket system. Another leak, at the other end of the summer, coming out of Dublin this time, suggests that in the first twenty-four hours the best way to deal with cross-border trade might just be to turn a blind eye.

support too among the business and farming communities, both of which, through their official bodies, are opposed to a no-deal Brexit. When a report in the first week of August suggested 45,000 cattle would be culled in the event of no deal, the Ulster Farmers Union queried the report's veracity but nevertheless said that no deal would be 'catastrophic' for their industry.)

Just how significantly trade would slow was highlighted by Northern Irish business leaders, back in June, in a discussion on BBC NI's *The View* that also included (from a studio in London) Kathy Gyngell, co-editor of *The Conservative Woman* (strapline: 'the philosophy, not the party'). There was – the local panel explained – the equivalent of a lorry crossing the border every six seconds. The average delay of ten minutes for a lorry crossing from Norway to Sweden – to take an example of a smooth trading arrangement that Brexit supporters often cited – was ten minutes. You didn't have to be a genius to do the maths.

Kathy Gyngell told them that with that sort of attitude, Britain would never have won two world wars. And the panel's faces, back in Belfast, as they looked at one another – whatever their individual politics, they were all in that moment Northern Irish.

Kathy Gyngell didn't stop there, which was her undoing. 'The fact that there is already a border for excise, duties, for... what else is there a border for...' – a quick look down at her notes, somewhere on the seat beside her, a clasping of her hands – 'I can't pretend I'm an expert on this, but it's not as though there aren't some checks that don't... VAT...'

And her face as she said that... I am back in school, 1977,

Additional Maths. The boy two desks back from me has just been asked the cosine of 42°: 0.582613457? Wrong: try again… 0.327481966? No, no, show me your log book. 'I forgot it, sir.' He's been guessing to nine decimal places. That was the face: caught out.

The starkest fact of all in Katy Hayward's article, taken straight from a Northern Ireland Civil Service report, is that 40,000 jobs could go in the event of a no-deal Brexit, or 5 per cent of the workforce. Even the DUP seems not to disagree, at least not about the figures. They maintain, though, that the problem is entirely of the EU's – and especially the Irish government's – making.

It's dead simple: remove the backstop, let the revised With-drawal Agreement pass through parliament, and then get down to the business of thrashing out a future trade agreement. Boris himself says, somewhat insouciantly, that the 40,000 figure is 'at the upper end' of projections. Which doesn't mean it isn't there, and even the lower end is still in the tens of thousands. And even this close to the thing (60 days, 9 hours and 33 minutes as I write that) there is no real sense that anyone, anywhere, is fully prepared for it actually coming to pass.

Everyone is agreed, we shouldn't be sacrificing other people's livelihoods for a principle, and everyone is equally agreed that they shouldn't be the ones to rise above theirs.

I can't remember now when I first heard Hong Kong mentioned.

Simon Coveney, the Irish Tánaiste, was already talking about it back at the end of 2017. 'I think,' he said then, 'there is probably no country in the world that defends its sovereign borders more aggressively than China does. Yet China lives with (and) functions with Hong Kong which has very much been part of Chinese territories, but operating under a different set of rules.' And then, shifting his tongue perhaps slightly towards his cheek: 'I'm not sure whether the Hong Kong solution is appropriate, for Northern Ireland or not, but it is an example, of ironically a British-designed solution.'

I had always understood that the status of present-day Hong Kong was actually dreamed up by former Chinese premier Deng Xiaoping, but maybe the solution was, as Simon Coveney said, British and only the slogan – 'one country, two systems' (echoes there of 'two schools, one roof') – Deng's. The *Hong Kong Free Press* picked up on Simon Coveney's comments, made, as it told its readers, 'while on a visit to a community centre in the Northern Ireland city of Belfast', which somehow puts us nicely, and very precisely, in our place. (It quoted too Boris Johnson – not yet PM–MU of course, but still Foreign Secretary – '[a return to a hard border] would be unthinkable, it would be economic and political madness. Everybody understands the social, political and spiritual ramifications.'[5])

Whether that speech of Simon Coveney's was what started it, or whether he was picking up on something that was already in the air, it seemed for a time to really catch on. There was always, in the Hong Kong analogy, when people invoked it here, an element of 'we would really rather Brexit wasn't happening at all, you understand, but if it absolutely has to, and we could be, you know, not quite in and not quite out...'

Not so much 'England's difficulty, Ireland's opportunity' as

'England, Wales and (against its will) Scotland's difficulty (not forgetting the rest of Ireland), Northern Ireland's opportunity'. Maybe, just maybe, we could benefit from all of this, rather than being beggared by it. (Our dilemma in a nutshell: Northern Ireland stands to gain most from the Withdrawal Agreement and to suffer most from No-Deal.)

A bit of me always suspected that some members at least of the DUP were alive to the possibilities for Northern Ireland of a slightly smudged or fudged future arrangement.* Katy Hayward – who has maintained a constant, at times it has seemed daily, commentary on the dangers inherent in a hard Brexit – said, back when the draft protocol was still inky-wet behind the ears, that a *soft* Brexit was not 'anathema to the DUP – in fact it is the conclusion to be drawn from its stated positions.' (Though not, as I say, stated anywhere that can easily be found on the Policies page of their website, unlike clear statements on the Implementation of the Military Covenant

---

* On fudge, my initial hope after the Referendum result was that the Conservative government would appoint only Northern Irish politicians to the negotiation team that they sent to Brussels and append the word 'Process' to Brexit. That way it would go on for years with long gaps where the whole thing was suspended, and shorter interludes where negotiators were travelling the world proclaiming it to be the Best Divorce Ever, while everyone else quietly forgot what it was we were processing from and processing to and simply rubbed along, until perhaps the centenary of the Referendum rolled around, at which point we would have some beautiful content of smiling, moderate-after-the-fact elder statespersons (150 by that stage being the new seventy-five) streamed onto our – possibly internal – 2116 screens. Instead, of course, Theresa May called an election and put a single Northern Irish party – the DUP – in charge of her government and the rest is...

and the Flying of the National Flag.) 'What is anathema to the DUP,' Katy Hayward continued, 'is the breakup of the UK. The best insurance against this happening is not a hard Brexit but properly functioning, heavy-duty devolution.'[6]

And still when it came to it, they voted against the Withdrawal Agreement, putting them doubly out of step (you're out of step, you shuffle your feet and you're still out of step) with the bulk of the Northern Ireland electorate who, having voted against Brexit, were strongly in favour of something very like Theresa May's deal. A December 2018 poll[7] put the support, evenly split between those who thought it was good for the economy here and those who simply thought it got around the problem of the border, at close to 65 per cent.[8]

This, as it happens, wasn't far off the percentage of Tory voters who, when polled, said they would prefer a Brexit that saw Northern Ireland leaving the Union over one that caused significant damage to the UK economy. It was cold comfort that the English voters – by a margin of 4 per cent – seemed to care for Scotland even less: a majority of the supporters of the party that the DUP were propping up through all of this were prepared to throw them under a bus... the big one with the £350 million plastered across the side of it, not the painted packing-case variety.*

---

* Here, my editor suggested cutting, saying: 'This already seems to have faded.' But I have left it in in response to those who cited it as evidence of Johnson's cunning: 'He said it so that when you Google *Boris Johnson, Bus*, you get this nonsense about him painting buses on boxes instead of the big Brexit lie.' You don't: you get the Brexit lie first, followed by 'conspiracy theory about Boris Johnson saying he paints buses...'

The day after the official launch of the Conservative Party leadership campaign, I was having a drink with a friend who told me he that he was a Hong-Konger. Or had been. 'Our economy is 70 per cent public money,' he said. That is the £10 billion 'block grant' from Westminster, plus the extra £1 billion extracted by the DUP in its confidence and supply deal. 'It needs to be 40 per cent or lower.' If Theresa May's deal had gone through we'd have had the best of both worlds: 'the money would have flowed in' – for a moment as he says it, I can almost see it. 'But,' he shakes his head, 'that's right off the table now.'

As happened in the past with frequently heard terms like 'draw a line under' and 'put beyond use', 'off the table' has leaped up the charts of late, knocking the previously unassailable 'not on the cards' off top spot.* It's not just the idiom of keeping things on the table – so beloved of No-Dealers – that has become popular, but the strategy too. Denis Bradley, the former Derry priest who went on to become a vice-chair of the Policing Board (and suffered at the hands – and baseball bats – of dissident republicans for it), as well co-chair of a Consultative Group on the Past, reflected in an interview in July on the possibility of a Border Poll: 'Of course it's the wrong time and it's crude, it's simplistic, and crude and wrong to have a border poll now. That's as crude as you can get. *The difficulty is that if you take that off the table, I'm not convinced unionism would move at all.'* (My emphasis.)[9]

---

* I nearly called my next novel *Iterations* after that word too leaked out of the world of draft agreements and into the everyday. As in the city-centre restaurant where I was handed what my server promised me was the latest iteration of the menu. (I think they used to call it Today's Specials.)

Talk of Border Polls has, historically, been a little more common here than talk of Hong Kong in the Irish Sea, though Brexit undoubtedly gave it renewed momentum. Sinn Féin, as might be expected, led the charge in calling for a United Ireland referendum – and it did sound for a while as though they were urging us on there at the gallop, although recent if not reversals then not-quite-as-dramatic as expected advances in other elections seemed to cause them to pull in the reins a bit and proceed at a more measured pace.

(Sorry, pausing there a moment: that was all getting too elaborate. Also I need to get the image out of my head of Terry Gilliam banging coconut shells together, as a bargain-basement steed, in *Monty Python and the Holy Grail*.)

Blogging in June, former Sinn Féin leader Gerry Adams said that a Border Poll without a plan would be plain stupid: witness the Brexit Referendum itself.[10] So no poll here, not today or tomorrow at least, but a conversation to be started, a plan of action put in place. Though, as some commentators have pointed out, since the Scottish parliament's White Paper on independence ran to some 670 pages, this is not a thing that, if it is done properly, is likely going to be done the day after tomorrow either. By which time, who can say…?

There have been plenty of voices cautioning against the assumption that unionists generally will, or would, be so traumatized by everything that has happened since June 2016 that they would be more easily persuaded than they had been up to now of the virtues of reunification. Eilis O'Hanlon in the *Daily Telegraph* wrote that '[i]magining that Brexit will blow a hole in unionists' entire identity is just another spasm of confirmation bias from people who never took the pro-Union community in Northern Ireland seriously in the first place.'[11]

But some clearly are thinking the previously unthinkable. Under the startling headline 'How Brexit changes a unionist to a United Irelander' (without surgery!), a former chair of the Londonderry [sic] Chamber of Commerce, Philip Gilliland, is quoted (on *Slugger O'Toole*, from an original podcast) as saying Brexit is a 'gift'. Why? '[B]ecause it's allowed those of us who are from a Protestant background to be able to talk about the heresy of the united Ireland in a way that is not heresy.' Time was, he says (echoing what my guide said on that Big Gay Tour of Belfast), Northerners – actually he's more specific and says unionists – saw themselves as more socially liberal and feared the influence of the Republic's 'theocracy'. Not any more: it is unionists themselves who are the theocrats these days. 'The idea of the socially conservative moral stuff coming out of unionism is utterly abhorrent to me. And frankly, ironically, rather un-British too.' He had only one caveat, a United Ireland couldn't be on Sinn Féin terms. 'If it's not under the aegis of Sinn Féin, I don't really care. I'm happy with it.'[12]

At the start of July, Northern Irish actor James Nesbitt announced that he was setting up a new campaign – Connected Citizens – to imagine, as he said, a 'new union of Ireland',[13] which instantly achieved something new in combining the two big shibboleths – 'the Union' and a 'United Ireland' – in one neat phrase, thereby neutralizing both. This came a couple of weeks after another of our leading actors, Adrian Dunbar, had spoken in *The Sun* about the advantages of an All-Ireland economy and the opportunities for investment that could come from the North staying in the UK *and* the EU. He had spoken too about pulling it into line with the rest of the country to become 'a forward thinking European democracy'. 'It's very difficult in this day and age,' he said, 'to imagine a place where politicians believe that homosexuality can be cured through psychoanalysis, and climate change is a quasi-religion and the earth is flat.'

Responding to Jimmy Nesbitt's initiative, Revd Mervyn Gibson, the Grand Secretary of the Orange Order, started off pretty much according to script. Here was another example of a famous Prod becoming squeamish about his background, feeling that it was on 'the wrong side of history'. But then Gibson said 'as a democrat' he was prepared to accept a United Ireland if that was the wish of the majority. 'I'm not,' he said, 'going to go to war over it.'[14]

These are all, of course, Northern voices. Quite what the South makes of it – of us – is another question, to which in recent months I have heard, or heard evidence of, different answers. 'They' – Southerners – 'haven't the first clue about this place.' This from a born-and-bred Dubliner in Belfast early in the summer with the Ireland Funds. 'They come up on raiding missions' – to the shops, he means, the exchange rate of late being much in their favour – 'and that's about it.' Unionism in particular is opaque to them. He would recommend taking Orange marches nation-, as in island-, wide: draw some of the sting out of them.

I always thought Dublin and London had more in common with one another than either had with Belfast, or anywhere else in the North, or the South for that matter. That relationship, though, feels as if it has ruptured. BBC Radio 4's *World at One* broadcasts an entire programme, the week of the fiftieth anniversary of the start of the Troubles, from Dublin and, first, from the County Cavan side of the border, where the Irish Finance Minister, Paschal Donohoe, repeats his government's and the EU's position that the backstop is not up for renegotiation: the backstop is there to guarantee that there will be no new border infrastructure. But, says the interviewer, if the British government, rejecting the backstop, pushes ahead with a no-deal Brexit, you'll end up with that infrastructure anyway, won't you. No, says Minister Donohoe. There will be no new infrastructure in the event of a no-deal Brexit either. Which is the cue for the next interviewee, the DUP's Sammy Wilson, who gets – as we like to say and as he loves to do – tore in. The backstop, he says, tears up the Belfast Agreement, which enshrines the principle of no change in the constitutional arrangement of Northern Ireland without the consent of a majority of its people. The backstop tears Northern Ireland out of the UK. Paschal Donohoe's interview proves the Irish government never had any intention of reinstating a border. No-deal will mean no checks. And off he goes, the DUP's version of the specialist kicker, job – in his and their eyes, no doubt – done.

Down in Dublin, Mark Lillis, a former diplomat in the Department of Foreign Affairs, reminds Radio 4's listeners that the normalization of British–Irish relations was of relatively short duration, really dating from the visit Queen Elizabeth made to Dublin in 2011, when she laid a wreath in the Garden of Remembrance to all who died in the cause of Irish freedom, and – having first addressed her hosts in Irish – spoke at a banquet in Dublin Castle of the 'heartache, turbulence, and loss' of the two islands' complex history, and the bonds, and the rapport – unimaginable a century before – that now existed between them.

Lillis characterizes affairs in post-Agreement Northern Ireland (Good Friday, he means, not St Andrews or Stormont or Fresh Start, whose names alone might bear out the point he is making) as 'a sequence of cycles where troubles begin and they get sorted out by Dublin and London'. Or did get sorted out. There is no community of purpose at all now between the two main parties up there. 'And if I may say,' he does say, 'it was a failure to recognize that' – on the part of Theresa May, cutting her deal with the DUP – 'that has led us to where we are.'

Mark Lillis was also one of three veterans of Irish–British relations who turned up the weekend before in the *Irish Times* talking again about what another of the trio, Séan Ó hUigínn, former joint secretary of the British–Irish Secretariat, refers to as 'the Black Swan of Brexit'. Ó hUigínn is if anything more jaundiced about the level of engagement, or basic understanding, of successive generations of British politicians: 'I think the great Mr Johnson – not Boris, but Samuel – said nothing odd lasts long. And what's happening [in] British politics now is so odd, it will not last long.'[15]

It's beautifully put, at the patrician end of the spectrum that includes those online gags showing the new range of British stamps: the hand holding a gun to a foot; the English bowman, bow bent, ready to unleash an arrow pointed at his own chest;

or the one (second class of course) showing Theresa May on UK Independence Day marching off the edge of a cliff backed by Boris on bass drum and ranks of bowler-hatted Orangemen. It is the British lot now to be lectured and lampooned. Well not the *British*, of course, just *them*, the Borises and the Nigels and the Jacob Double-Barrelleds, the maybe not-so-bumbling toffs, but there is too here and there a little bit of nudge-nudge collateral, across the water and maybe up the road.

I am reminded of a text from an English friend living in Belfast at the time of the 2017 election: 'I don't like the DUP – OBVIOUSLY – but is it me or is there some nasty anti-NI-ism lurking in the English coverage?' It isn't – wasn't him.

A man I've met before comes up to me during the interval of an event I am taking part in in County Meath. He tells me in not much more than an undertone (we are in a decommissioned church: it encourages the lowered voice) that everybody down here is talking as though a United Ireland is just around the corner. 'There's a green groupthink,' he says, and gives me instances of what he sees as carelessness and insensitivity in public discourse. As he is talking to me, I am remembering that the week before, down south again, or actually out west, I had heard a man, an academic, explain to an American visitor that English was not 'our' language and that the reason 'we Irish' became so creative in our use of English was defensive, to keep ourselves from being swamped entirely.

This is a Littler Ireland than I have heard in a while. The most recent *Faber Book of Irish Short Stories*, edited by Lucy Caldwell and featuring only writers (from North and South) who began publishing after the Good Friday Agreement, is called – gloriously – *Being Various*.* English is our language as well as Irish. So is Polish. So is Sign (Irish, Northern Irish and British). So are Punjabi and Arabic and Mandarin Chinese. When you say 'We Irish', you mean 'Some of us Irish' or even just 'Me Irish'.

And I'm happy for you in my own Irish way.

In the course of the interview in the *Irish Times*, Séan Ó hUigínn talks of it having been the secret hope of those who worked on the Good Friday Agreement that a united Ireland if or when it comes on the agenda will do so against a background of a 'Northern Ireland, you know, not being a failed entity, so to speak.' Now? 'I think that hope is gone.'[16]

Off the table, you might almost say. Our not being a failure.

As the summer progresses, meanwhile, the special administrative region of Hong Kong in the South China Sea edges closer to confrontation with China, suggesting there might be a limit to the lifespan of the one-territory-two-systems model. In the week of the fiftieth anniversary of the introduction of troops here, in fact, Hong Kong looks more like we once did than we look like it, a sort of administrative-region-sized version of Dorian Gray.

It's all a very long way from the phoney-war months immediately after the Referendum. Early in 2017, I drove around the South Armagh border with the photographer Donovan Wylie

---

* The title, like the title of the 'More of it Than we Think' documentary I once made, is from 'Snow' by Belfast-born Louis MacNeice, a 1935 poem that has acquired the status almost of national lyric for a younger generation of writers: 'I peel and portion a tangerine and spit the pips and feel / The drunkenness of things being various.' We have a magazine called the *Tangerine* too.

for a *Guardian* article on how Brexit was affecting communities there. This was before Theresa May called *that* election, when it seemed not unreasonable to expect that she might be going to Brussels to negotiate from a position of strength within her own party and parliament.

In an area known for its strong support of Irish republicanism, with signs everywhere warning of road closures in the event of a hard Brexit, the views I heard expressed were more varied than might perhaps have been expected. Time and again, I wrote, I was cheered by the thought that pragmatism would always triumph over ideology. As Donovan and I were about to get into the car for the final time to drive back to Belfast, a man sidled up to me. 'There's always a border,' he told me. 'It's just a question of what you can get up and down the road.'

There is no shortage of humour even now. One of my favourite gags is a graphic showing two yellow-headed characters, super-heroed up, striding towards one another across grass divided by a broad white line. (Ireland's most popular crisp, you need to know, is Tayto: but there is a Northern version and a Southern.)

'Both Mr Taytos meet at the former Irish border upon reunification,' runs the legend, 'to determine who becomes Ireland's one true crisp.'

But there is much, too, that makes you just want to stay in bed some mornings and pull the covers over your head in hopes that it all just goes away.

★

So, let me fly you back to the other end of the summer, the second week of June. It's been raining quite a bit. (It's not the amount of rain here that irks, it's that it tends to fall at times when weather forecasters standing before their green screens in London are telling the rest of the UK not to leave home without sunblock.) A Tuesday night, the Sunflower Bar on Union Street. The Sunflower sits on a corner, one block along from the edge of what we can now without exaggeration call Belfast's gay quarter, a couple of blocks in the other direction from the former Smithfield market. It will soon be overtaken by development – Ulster University's newly expanded Belfast campus is filling in many of the spaces (and making a few spaces to fill) around it. For now, though, it is to an extent a world unto itself, boasting one of the last surviving examples of Troubles-era security apparatus: a 'cage' around its front door, which is, as it would never have been in that Troubles era, left open during business hours. (Standing outside one of those cages, waiting for the bar staff, watching on the security monitor, to size you up – literally – was a rite of passage for underage drinkers in the 1970s and 1980s. The trick, always, was to push your beardiest, or most heavily made-up, friend to the fore.) On one side of the bar, Library Street rises towards Carrick Hill. Just walking up it in the old days would have been enough to identify you as Catholic, a 'fact' that loyalist assassins – most notoriously, the Shankill Butchers gang – exploited on any number of occasions, as Lyra McKee noted in 'Suicide of the Ceasefire Babies', recalling a night she ended up in the Sunflower, 'drinking, at a table with my Protestant best friend, at least two republicans and a group of Corbynite socialists. Times have changed. If I'd been born a decade earlier, I wouldn't have dared to venture down those streets, never mind drink there. Now, it's safe.'

This particular night, as I approach, the Sunflower's owner Pedro Donald is waiting outside with his partner. Award-winning bar staff from all over the world are arriving, having earlier been at the Bushmills Whiskey Distillery, deep in *Game of Thrones* territory. This is part of their prize. A band is tuning up behind the palings of the beer garden. I feel Eagles circling. But I am headed for the upstairs bar, which – a few years before Pedro moved in and Sunflowered it – stood in without much need for set-dressing (which, given the budget the producers were working with was just as well) for a 1970s bar frequented by paramilitaries in *Good Vibrations*, and which tonight is playing host to the launch of the latest in the 'Lifeboat' series of poetry pamphlets.

The Lifeboat's name derives from a poem in Michael Longley's 2011 collection, *A Hundred Doors*, which laments the passing of another landlord, Charlie Gaffney, but maybe owes something too to the fact that its first home was a restaurant in a barge moored on the River Lagan behind the Waterfront Hall. (*Confiance*, the barge is named: Trust.)

I make it up the stairs just in time. Stephen Connolly, who runs the Lifeboat with his partner Manuela Moser, is about to make his way to the mic to start proceedings. 'The Lifeboat,' he says, by way of welcome, 'is often cited as representing a new Belfast.' Their original model was to team an unpublished writer with a published one, have a reading, publish a pamphlet by the (thereafter-no-longer) unpublished writer, limited run, fifty copies, pound apiece. Enough to go again. They're still doing that regularly but, though Stephen and Manuela are still students themselves, they are now a fully established commercial press too. The pamphlets being launched tonight by Scott McKendry and Caitlin Newby – the former from here, the latter from LA – are the seventh and eighth they have done in just a couple of years. 'We don't strive to represent a new anything, to do so would be futile and self-indulgent.' He pauses, smiles, 'but even so…'

Even so.

Scott McKendry is first up competing with the Eagles, who have as suspected landed – all Lyin' Eyes and thin disguise – in the beer garden. It is in the introduction to one of his poems that he says the thing that I quote at the start of this book, about where we live being a piss-take of the world. The laughter in the room – from the mainly twenty- and thirty-year-olds in the audience – strikes me almost as much as the line itself: instant recognition.*

It's only on my way back out that I notice that on the hoardings that surround one of the about-to-be building sites on Library Street – for the moment a gallery of Belfast street art – is a new portrait of Lyra McKee – her black-and-white (though smiling, and bright) image offset by the small cluster of flowers in pots and jars – in one case, a yellow mug – on the pavement, where her waist meets the ground.

---

* When I bump into Scott again the next night, I ask him whether I had heard him right. He laughs and tells me that, later, back at a friend's house with others from the Lifeboat, he had wondered about that line himself: 'Where did that come from?' Two days after that again a new poem arrives in my inbox. Scott. It is no spoiler to tell you the gist of the last line.

Though hard to pick out at first, her 'letter to my fourteen-year-old self' is written in full on the panels either side of her portrait, two sentences pulled out and up and painted in white capitals: IT WON'T ALWAYS BE LIKE THIS. IT'S GOING TO GET BETTER.

I had only been told a few days before about the decision by the Ireland Funds to give their forty-seventh annual literary award to Lyra and – in her memory, and with her partner's blessing – our Fighting Words Belfast charity. The ceremony takes place (I flew you back, now I'm sliding you forward) on Midsummer's Eve, in – of all places, I'm thinking to myself in advance – St Anne's Cathedral, made over for the night into an enormous, vaulted function room.

It's a busy night in Belfast. If festivals are your thing, it's pretty nearly always a busy night in Belfast – or day: even the Twelfth now is (has been for more than a decade) Orangefest.

Tonight, Ben Nicky is appearing at the Belsonic music festival in Custom House Square, while round in the Belfast Harbour Commissioners Office, on the city centre's northern edge, the world's largest literary festival – Jaipur Literature Festival – is launching its first ever mini JLF in Belfast: 'Each Other's Stories'. I work out I can have about half an hour there before having to leave for the Ireland Funds dinner. This, as it turns out, is enough time to see Mahatma Gandhi's grand-daughter, Tara Gandhi Bhattacharjee, arrive. She's eighty-five, but with her hair in a high bun, she has a look about her and the poise of Audrey Hepburn. And coming in just behind her is Arlene Foster, but already I am through the doors and a festival volunteer is tying a bracelet of coloured twine, four small pewter bells attached, onto my right wrist. 'For happiness,' she says.

Then with fellow writer Lucy Caldwell – another Fighting Words supporter – I hightail it out of there, on foot, back into town, through the crowds making their way to Custom House Square, to St Anne's Cathedral.

Where we are early.

For maybe half an hour, in the cathedral, just the catering staff and us and Emily DeDakis from Fighting Words, and one of the teenage writers who has been going along to a young playwrights course – the Right Twig – Emily has been running, and who is going to say a few words – about the benefits of the course, of Fighting Words Belfast – when the award is made.

And, of course, I am remembering the last time I was in this cathedral, a shade under two months before, and wondering how anything even vaguely celebratory – in Lyra McKee's name – can possibly take place here so soon. But the room gradually fills with members of the Ireland Funds and their invited guests and Lyra's partner, Sarah Canning, arrives, from Derry, with her sister, and we all sit to eat, to drink, to talk, and then pause to listen to speeches.

The Ireland Funds outgoing chair, hotelier John Fitzpatrick, gives special thanks to Arlene Foster for her ongoing support for the Funds' charitable activities – he gestures with his hand towards where she is sitting, and that is the first I know she is there – sitting front and centre – having obviously left the JLF launch after Lucy and I did.

At one point between courses and just before the announcement of the award, I go to the bathroom, pausing at the bar (there's a full bar in the cathedral!) to talk to one – Irish-based – Ireland Funds delegate who I met the previous day at a Fighting Words workshop. He tells me that the US members are particularly exercised by what they consider the slow progress here of integrated education, an area that they have been supporting for quite a number of years now. 'They say to me,' he says to me, '"It's at 8 per cent? Is that all?" I say to them, "All? It's a fucking miracle it's that high!"' He tells me too that they are desperate to do something in Derry, which is where Fighting Words could come in.

When I make my way back eventually, Arlene Foster is standing at the Fighting Words table, next to Sarah Canning's chair, talking. It would be rude to eavesdrop but it would be impossible for anyone present not to pick up a few words of what passes – in a friendly way – between them, about the fact that Lyra and Sarah were of different religions, that they used to get a bit of stick for it, but that it had never been any sort of an issue for the two of them.

When she was Minister for Enterprise, Arlene Foster sent me a message congratulating Colin Carberry and me on a nomination we had got for a BAFTA for *Good Vibrations*, and as she finishes her conversation with Sarah Canning, she says hello. I hear the not-quite jingle of pewter bells. She's wearing a happiness bracelet. 'Snap,' I say and show her mine. She asks if I was still at the launch when Tara Gandhi Bhattacharjee spoke. No? Well, she had said how honoured she was to be in the land of Yeats, Oscar Wilde, Seamus Heaney and... Bobby Sands.

Arlene mimics her own expression, there in the Harbour Commissioners, eyes widening, but still smiling... 'And she didn't just say it once, she said it three times. And, of course,' she tells me, 'Máirtín Ó Muilleoir' – former Sinn Féin Finance Minister and Lord Mayor of Belfast, and one-man social media platform – 'is filming the whole thing.' I tell her I am sorry I missed it, but on second thoughts I am glad I did, so that I got to hear her tell me the story, and hear her laugh, at herself.

I disagree fundamentally with Arlene Foster's politics and I rarely warm to her when I see her on TV or hear her on radio, but she is a pleasant person to talk to. I remember my mum and dad meeting Martin McGuinness at a photography exhibition by the late John Harrison – different generations of the same family (a photo in among the many of Martin McGuinness and his mother, one of me with my gran in the Linen Hall Library). They shook his hand, chatted. My dad, whose brother had been shot by the IRA in Derry, then under Martin McGuinness's command. You take people as you find them... I think too of this summer, when the Northern Irish producers of Alex Gibney's documentary *No Stone Unturned* walked out of a Belfast court after the police case against them was dropped. Standing behind, shoulder to shoulder with their solicitor, the new Lord Mayor of Belfast, John Finucane of Sinn Féin (whose father Pat was murdered by loyalists with the connivance of the RUC), was none other than David Davis, former Tory Brexit Secretary, white-haired bête-noire of Remain voters. People who support things you don't like sometimes like – and support – things you do.

Sarah Canning, receiving Lyra's award, is dignity and strength of character personified. She makes no mention of the fact that the last time she was here was for Lyra's funeral. Arlene Foster by this time is in her seat at a table not more than a handful of yards from where she sat that day, with other politicians, a split second after the rest of the congregation rose to their feet. It doesn't in the circumstances feel like my place to mention it either. This is a moment for looking forward.

I ask the young writer from the Right Twig up to give his first-hand testimony of the virtues of Fighting Words and realize, just from the way he takes the mic from me and sets himself, that this isn't someone to whom a few words come naturally. Words, yes, but *few*...? He takes one – long – look into the room, at all those businesspeople and politicians, then smiles and says that he seems to be by some distance the youngest person there. He talks – freestyles – a while, about the very fact that he is young and has much to say, about the fact that he is young, has much to say and is up there saying it and who can stop him... He's bringing the house down. I think he might be weighing up whether to do a full set – but then he smiles again. He's said all he wants to say for now.

'I love you all,' he tells them in parting. 'Peace.'

At time of writing (friendship bracelet just about hanging in there), things here look fifty shades short of rosy in the short and even medium term. The parliamentary battle is about to resume just as I leave off. By the time you are reading this, the backstop may be as dead as Bebo. I could be emailing eBay sellers to tell them that a hard border does not mean they have to charge extra for postage.

Or something may yet occur that prevents a no-deal Brexit – any form of Brexit. I sincerely hope that it does, and that, in the event of no Brexit at all, genuine efforts are made to address the feelings of alienation that were clearly a factor in many millions of people, not all of whom were dupes or xenophobes or pining for lost Empire, voting to leave in the first place.

And if we do go, there is just as big a job – perhaps even bigger – to be done among those who wanted to remain, or to leave, if leave they had to, on a very different basis. More than anything I hope that the only wounds that need to be healed are emotional, here above all, where this whole enterprise still looks as though it will stand or fall.

To my 1.87 million fellow citizens… what the Right Twigger says.

Look Up (Postscript)

The things you don't know you don't know.

Lyra McKee was named for the constellation which lies on the edge of the Milky Way, and which in turn takes its name from the lyre of Orpheus.

When he was torn limb from limb, Orpheus's lyre fell into a river and was retrieved by an eagle sent by Apollo. His head fell into the sea and was carried on the waves to the shores of Lesbos.

In some versions of the myth, when the Maenads who murdered him try to wash the blood from their hands in the river, the waters recede, and keep receding with each new attempt, which – whether it was in their minds or not – calls to mind the actions of Lyra McKee's friends, placing red hands on the wall of Junior McDaid House, hangout of her murderer's political wing.

Lyra, the constellation, is famous for its meteor showers, the Lyrids – according to NASA, among the oldest for which records exist, as far back as the 680s BC. The showers occur at more or less the same time every year between 16 and 26 April. The NASA viewing tips read like a life lesson:

The Lyrids are best viewed in the Northern Hemisphere during the dark hours (after moonset and before dawn). Find an area well away from city or street lights. Come prepared with a sleeping bag, blanket or lawn chair. Lie flat on your back with your feet facing east and look up, taking in as much of the sky as possible. After about 30 minutes in the dark, your eyes will adapt and you will begin to see meteors. Be patient – the show will last until dawn, so you have plenty of time to catch a glimpse.[1]

And we're talking Northern Ireland, and we're talking April, we're talking night, but in fact if we were looking for a way to remember all who have died down the years here while reflecting on our place in the cosmos, we could do a lot worse next Lyrid season than to take ourselves off somewhere for half an hour and wait for the lights.

—Belfast, September 2019

Acknowledgements

My thanks, first, foremost, to Ali FitzGibbon, and to Jessica and Miranda Patterson; to Rachel Brown and to Richard English; to Damian Smyth, who not for the first time reminded me of a couple of things of which I badly needed reminding; to the many people I spoke to across the months of writing who were kind enough to allow me to use their words. And to Elaine Gaston and Scott McKendry, very particularly, for their words.

Thanks to Clare Gordon at Head of Zeus and finally, to my editor, Neil Belton, who first suggested this book and whose encouragement throughout has been invaluable.

We have three excellent daily newspapers in Northern Ireland – the *Belfast Telegraph*, the *Irish News* and the *News Letter*. I refer often to all three, and to the *Slugger O'Toole* portal, which not only offers a platform to commentators of all political opinions but draws its readers' attention to stories and articles they might otherwise (and I certainly would have) missed.

Notes

Front Matter

1 www.telegraph.co.uk/politics/2019/07/26/dear-prime-minister-please-tread-carefully-handling-irish-border

Up to Speed

1 Devlin, Anne, 'Responsibility for the Dead', in *Irish Pages: The Belfast Agreement Twentieth Anniversary Issue.*
2 Carmel McCafferty was being interviewed on Radio Ulster's *Talkback* on 12 August 2019.
3 www.bbc.co.uk/news/uk-northern-ireland-48626564

DUP

1 cain.ulster.ac.uk/events/peace/talks.htm
2 www.belfasttelegraph.co.uk/news/northern-ireland/united-ireland-acceptable-to-eileen-paisley-if-there-is-freedom-of-religion-38149393.html
3 www.hotpress.com/music/in-this-issue-of-hot-pressfree-content-2927817
4 www.belfastlive.co.uk/news/belfast-news/sammy-wilson-dup-brexit-food-15750704

5   www.belfasttelegraph.co.uk/news/politics/sammy-wilson-goes-from-figure-of-fun-to-principal-player-28543278.html

6   www.nuzhound.com/articles/Sunday_Tribune/arts2007/mar4_Shinners_Sharon_unrepentant_Republican__SBreen.php

7   www.belfasttelegraph.co.uk/news/northern-ireland/iris-robinson-damned-by-report-guilty-of-serious-breach-of-assembly-code-30783463.html

What a Carve-up/Up the Hill

1   sluggerotoole.com/2019/06/12/micheal-martin-time-for-those-elected-to-serve-in-democratic-institutions-to-be-allowed-to-get-to-work

2   www.belfasttelegraph.co.uk/news/northern-ireland/dungannon-farmer-is-biggest-rhi-claimant-with-13-boilers-running-35538815.html

3   www.irishtimes.com/news/ireland/irish-news/eamonn-mallie-a-way-for-arlene-foster-to-redeem-herself-1.3000191

4   www.belfasttelegraph.co.uk/news/northern-ireland/parts-of-draft-agreement-between-dup-and-sinn-fein-leaked-36624722.html

5   sluggerotoole.com/2019/07/12/abortion-and-marriage-equality-amendments-should-ensure-a-key-aim-of-the-northern-ireland-bill-fails

Up the Ra

1   www.youtube.com/watch?v=BAfF7o2jgn4 (c. 6'05")

2   mosaicscience.com/story/conflict-suicide-northern-ireland

3   www.bbc.co.uk/news/uk-northern-ireland-49357887

4 www.belfasttelegraph.co.uk/sunday-life/lyra-mckee-murder-suspect-set-to-be-a-dad-teens-baby-conceived-same-week-of-fatal-shooting-38391721.html

5 theconversation.com/northern-ireland-how-some-of-the-agreement-generation-are-drawn-into-paramilitary-groups-116033

6 www.belfasttelegraph.co.uk/news/northern-ireland/saoradh-leader-says-continuation-of-dissident-republican-violence-inevitable-38442074.html

7 www.bbc.com/news/uk-northern-ireland-48997405

8 www.irishnews.com/news/northernirelandnews/2019/05/10/news/east-belfast-cultural-collective-established-to-support-smaller-eleventh-night-bonfires-targeted-by-authorities--1616563

9 www.bbc.co.uk/news/uk-northern-ireland-49234364

10 www.irishtimes.com/news/crime-and-law/north-desensitised-to-extreme-violence-conference-told-1.2456091

Cupar Street

1 www.theguardian.com/uk/gallery/2012/jan/22/belfast-peace-wall

2 www.belfasttelegraph.co.uk/news/northern-ireland/vow-to-remove-peace-walls-by-2023-29254818.html

3 www.ted.com/talks/lyra_mckee_in_memory_of/transcript

4 share.transistor.fm/s/bbb0f72f

Up to Two a Day

1 www.bbc.co.uk/news/world-europe-49152264

2 www.bbc.co.uk/news/uk-scotland-scotland-business-49316478

Uppa Queers

1 news.bbc.co.uk/1/hi/uk/4543142.stm
2 www.belfastlive.co.uk/whats-on/arts-culture-news/gilbert--george-talk-belfast-14198897
3 qubsinnfein.wordpress.com/2014/10/20/malachai-ohara-queer-eye-for-a-new-ireland
4 www.bbc.co.uk/news/av/uk-northern-ireland-49194678/lgbtq-northern-ireland-i-have-never-experienced-any-hate-crime

Up and Down the Road

1 www.belfasttelegraph.co.uk/life/features/why-bishop-of-clogher-wrote-to-boris-johnson-over-brexit-and-his-fears-for-the-irish-border-38434783.html
2 www.irishtimes.com/opinion/diarmaid-ferriter-british-indifference-to-irish-border-is-indefensible-1.3476553
3 www.irishtimes.com/opinion/no-deal-brexit-moves-from-fantasy-machismo-into-stark-reality-1.3954889
4 fullfact.org/europe/irish-border-trade
5 www.hongkongfp.com/2017/11/23/irish-minister-suggests-hong-kong-style-deal-post-brexit-northern-ireland
6 qpol.qub.ac.uk/protocol-ireland-northern-ireland
7 www.prospectmagazine.co.uk/politics/three-reasons-the-irish-toptop-is-actually-a-good-thing
8 docs.wixstatic.com/ugd/024943_b89b42d32364461298ba5fe7867d82e1.pdf
9 sluggerotoole.com/2019/07/19/brexit-means-that-northern-irelands-constitutional-future-has-become-an-issue-for-europe-says-denis-bradley
10 sluggerotoole.com/2019/06/09/adams-a-referendum-without-a-plan-is-stupid

11 www.telegraph.co.uk/politics/2019/07/31/sinn-fein-will-bitterly-disappointed-think-brexit-will-lead

12 sluggerotoole.com/2019/06/21/how-brexit-changes-a-unionist-to-a-united-irelander

13 www.belfasttelegraph.co.uk/news/northern-ireland/james-nesbitt-wants-new-union-of-ireland-as-he-reveals-project-to-give-voice-to-silent-majority-38287899.html

14 www.belfasttelegraph.co.uk/news/northern-ireland/orange-order-chief-will-accept-united-ireland-if-majority-votes-for-it-38298886.html

15 www.irishtimes.com/news/politics/britain-has-always-struggled-to-take-ireland-seriously-say-irish-ex-diplomats-1.3981993

16 ibid.

Look Up (Postscript)

1   solarsystem.nasa.gov/asteroids-comets-and-meteors/meteors-and-meteorites/lyrids/in-depth

About the Author

GLENN PATTERSON was born and lives in Belfast. He has written a number of acclaimed novels and co-wrote the screenplay of the film *Good Vibrations*, based on the Belfast music scene of the 1970s. He is Director of the Seamus Heaney Centre at Queen's University.